A Guide to

FOOD BUYING IN JAPAN

A Guide to
FOOD BUYING
IN JAPAN

by Carolyn R. Krouse

4 901054 200063

CHARLES E. TUTTLE COMPANY
Rutland · Vermont : Tokyo · Japan

Published by the Charles E. Tuttle Company, Inc.
of Rutland, Vermont & Tokyo, Japan
with editorial offices at
Suido 1-chome, 2–6, Bunkyo-ku, Tokyo

Library of Congress Catalog Card No. 86–50702
International Standard Book No. 0–8048–1503–8

First printing, 1986
Fourth printing, 1989

Printed in Japan

⋊ TABLE OF CONTENTS

TABLES

✂ PREFACE

This book has been written with the intention of taking some of the mystery and expense out of shopping for food in Japan. My hope has been to create a handbook small enough to carry to the food market but complete enough to help the person who does not read Japanese to make informed decisions about most food and household purchases.

Food floors, found usually at the basement level of major department stores, offer opportunities for you to become familiar with the wide variety of foods available. Sales counters there provide taste samples, complete with toothpicks to be used as forks and plastic bags for their disposal. There is also a large selection of pre-cooked take-out foods such as fried fish and chicken, salads, Chinese-style dishes, and many other items. At little expense, then, it is possible to learn to identify products found in local shops and supermarkets, and to explore dishes worth incorporating into daily menus or ordering in restaurants.

Because markets in Japan carry an astonishing array of products, a comprehensive book on the subject of food buying would be too bulky to carry to the market. As a result, some traditional Japanese foods and some easily found Western foods are not discussed in this book. Readers interested in learning more about traditional foods will find many books on the subject. The Recommended Reading section lists a few of them.

I am greatly indebted to the many persons who helped in this project, particularly to Harold Krouse, Nobuko Fuku-chi, and Linda Sanders, whose kind support and skillful assistance continued throughout the preparation of this book. I would also like to thank Diane Robert, my mother, who taught me by example that the foods of other cultures will reward the person who explores them.

PART II

BEFORE YOU SHOP

1 · READING AND PRONOUNCING JAPANESE

Some portions of food labels in Japan may be written in the Roman alphabet, called *rōmaji* in Japanese, but most labels are written in the Japanese writing system, which is composed of Chinese characters, or *kanji,* and two syllabaries, *hiragana* and *katakana.*

KANJI

The oldest form of Japanese writing came to Japan from China. An individual Chinese character is called a kanji; this term is also used for characters collectively. What distinguishes kanji from most other writing systems is that the characters represent meaning as well as sound. Each character was originally derived from a picture representing an object or a concept, but over the centuries the characters became much more abstract and abbreviated.

In Japanese, there are usually several possible pronunciations, or readings, for a given character. For example, the character 米 can be read *kome, mai,* or *bei.* Some readings of a character are used when it appears alone: 米 alone is read *kome* and means "(uncooked) rice." Other readings are generally used in compound words: *mai* and *bei* are found in, for example, 玄米 *gemmai,* "brown (unrefined) rice," and 米価 *beika,* "the price of rice." (To complicate matters, the reading *kome* may be used in certain compounds as well.) Among words containing a given character, the correct reading of that character in each word must be memorized.

A single character can represent a word of one syllable (酢 *su,* vinegar) or several syllables (魚 *sakana,* fish). Since kanji represent concepts, one can often guess the meaning of a word if one knows the meaning of the kanji that make it up, even if the pronunciations to be used in the particular case are not known.

For the person who does not read kanji and does not know whether one character represents a word or a partial word, it is important to know that on food labels, individual words are separated from one another by a diagonal slash, a raised dot, or a space. This method is used in particular in the space for the list of ingredients.

TABLE 1: Hiragana and Katakana Syllabaries

a あ ア	i い イ	u う ウ	e え エ	o お オ
ka か カ	ki き キ	ku く ク	ke け ケ	ko こ コ
sa さ サ	shi し シ	su す ス	se せ セ	so そ ソ
ta た タ	chi ち チ	tsu つ ツ	te て テ	to と ト
na な ナ	ni に ニ	nu ぬ ヌ	ne ね ネ	no の ノ
ha は ハ	hi ひ ヒ	fu ふ フ	he へ ヘ	ho ほ ホ
ma ま マ	mi み ミ	mu む ム	me め メ	mo も モ
ya や ヤ		yu ゆ ユ		yo よ ヨ
ra ら ラ	ri り リ	ru る ル	re れ レ	ro ろ ロ
wa わ ワ				o を ヲ
~n ん ン				
ga が ガ	gi ぎ ギ	gu ぐ グ	ge げ ゲ	go ご ゴ
za ざ ザ	ji じ ジ	zu ず ズ	ze ぜ ゼ	zo ぞ ゾ
da だ ダ	(ji ぢ ヂ)	(zu づ ヅ)	de で デ	do ど ド
ba ば バ	bi び ビ	bu ぶ ブ	be べ ベ	bo ぼ ボ
pa ぱ パ	pi ぴ ピ	pu ぷ プ	pe ぺ ペ	po ぽ ポ

Note: For each syllable, the hiragana appears on the left, the katakana on the right.

KANA

Hiragana and katakana, referred to collectively as *kana*, are symbols that represent the sound of a single syllable (e.g., *a, ka, kya*). In this respect, kana differ from the letters of the alphabet, each of which generally represents a single sound. Unlike kanji, kana have no meaning in themselves. There are forty-six symbols in each syllabary; these are shown in the upper left section of Table 1 below. As shown in the bottom half of the Table, the symbol ＂ written to the upper right of a kana symbol "converts" a voiceless consonant to a voiced one (e.g., *k* to *g*), and the symbol °

and Sound Combinations

kya	きゃ	キャ	kyu	きゅ	キュ	kyo	きょ	キョ
sha	しゃ	シャ	shu	しゅ	シュ	sho	しょ	ショ
cha	ちゃ	チャ	chu	ちゅ	チュ	cho	ちょ	チョ
nya	にゃ	ニャ	nyu	にゅ	ニュ	nyo	にょ	ニョ
hya	ひゃ	ヒャ	hyu	ひゅ	ヒュ	hyo	ひょ	ヒョ
mya	みゃ	ミャ	myu	みゅ	ミュ	myo	みょ	ミョ
rya	りゃ	リャ	ryu	りゅ	リュ	ryo	りょ	リョ
gya	ぎゃ	ギャ	gyu	ぎゅ	ギュ	gyo	ぎょ	ギョ
ja	じゃ	ジャ	ju	じゅ	ジュ	jo	じょ	ジョ
(ja	ぢゃ	ヂャ)	(ju	ぢゅ	ヂュ)	(jo	ぢょ	ヂョ)
bya	びゃ	ビャ	byu	びゅ	ビュ	byo	びょ	ビョ
pya	ぴゃ	ピャ	pyu	ぴゅ	ピュ	pyo	ぴょ	ピョ

The following combinations are found in words of foreign origin only: ti ティ, di ディ, che チェ, fa ファ, fi フィ, wi ウィ.

in the same position "converts" an *h*-sound to a *p*-sound. When the small symbols ゃ/ャ, ゅ/ュ, and ょ/ョ are written immediately after a regular-sized symbol (right side of the Table), the two sounds represented by the symbols are blended into a single syllable.

The form of each kana symbol is much simpler than that of most kanji. Hiragana are rounded and curved, while katakana are angular. With experience, one can easily distinguish between the two syllabaries themselves and between each syllabary and kanji.

Because kana represent sound only, it is possible to sound out a word written in one of the syllabaries and then refer to a Japanese–English dictionary in which the entry words are romanized. Japanese–English dictionaries in which the entry words are in kana also exist; in fact, these are more common than romanized dictionaries.

Any word written in kanji can be written out in kana (for example, the words related to rice on page 13 may be written as follows: *kome,* こめ or コメ; *gemmai,* げんまい or ゲンマイ; *beika,* べいか or ベイカ). However, the kanji and the syllabaries have separate functions.

Kanji are used to represent nouns, verbs, and adjectives. Hiragana have various functions, but with respect to food labels, this syllabary is used to write words native to the Japanese language for which no kanji exists or for which the kanji is considered outmoded or too difficult. Even when a certain kanji is in current use, however, a food packager may at his discretion use hiragana to represent the word. In other words, different firms, markets, etc., are not always consistent in their use of kanji and hiragana for, say, the generic name of a certain product. A further complication is that a compound word may be written half in hiragana, half in kanji.

Katakana are used for foreign-derived words, for example, ビタミン *bitamin,* "vitamin." Compounds of foreign and Japanese words are written in mixed katakana–kanji (e.g., ポリ袋, *pori-bukuro,* polybag); combinations of katakana and hiragana are also possible. Finally, katakana may occasionally be used instead of hiragana, often for an emphatic effect. A food label can thus appear with all three elements of the Japanese writing system, as well as an occasional word in the Roman or another alphabet.

ROMANIZATION AND PRONUNCIATION

Table 1 also shows the system of romanization (basically the Hepburn system) used throughout this book for the transcription of Japanese words. The following paragraphs discuss the pronunciation and romanization of Japanese, and explain in more detail the kana syllabaries, where appropriate.

The five vowels of Japanese can be pronounced as follows:

> *a* as in "father"   (not as in "apple")
> *i* as in "machine"
> *u* as in "put"
> *e* as in "set"
> *o* as in "old"

A macron over a vowel indicates that the vowel is to be pronounced with the same sound as an ordinary vowel but is to be held about doubly long (e.g., *batā,* butter; *kyūri,* cucumber; *bēkon,* bacon; *budō,* grape). For a long *i,* the vowel is doubled rather than shown with a macron (e.g., *serorii,* celery). In katakana, a long vowel is represented by a dash — (e.g., バター for *batā,* セロリー for *serorii,* ベーコン

for *bēkon*). In hiragana, a long *a, i,* or *u* is shown by adding the characters あ, い, or う, respectively (e.g., きゅうり for *kyūri*). A long *o* is almost always shown by adding う, not, as might be expected, お (e.g., ぶどう for *budō*).

Most consonant sounds in Japanese are similar enough to those of English so that the use of English consonant sounds will usually result in one's being understood. *G* is always pronounced hard, as in "give" and "get." *Ts* may be difficult to pronounce when it comes at the beginning of words; it sounds like the *ts* of "catsup." The Japanese *r* should be pronounced like the British-English *r* in "very." When the *r* comes at the beginning of a word (e.g., *roppyaku,* 600), a short *d*-sound can be substituted with a surprising amount of success.

When two like consonants appear in succession, as in *gappi,* "the date," the consonant sound should be held doubly long. In this example, saying the *p*-sound quickly (as in the English word "happy") would result in an incorrect pronunciation. In kana, the double consonant is symbolized by a small っ or ッ before the symbol containing the consonant sound to be doubled. For example, *gappi* could be written がっぴ or ガッピ.

When an *n* appears at the end of a word (e.g., *bēkon,* bacon) or before an apostrophe (e.g., *gen'en,* low salt), it is pronounced somewhat like the *n* of the French word *bon,* rather than like an ordinary *n*. This "syllabic *n*" is represented by the hiragana ん (げんえん for *gen'en*) and in katakana by ン (ベーコン for *bēkon*). This ん/ン is romanized *m* when it appears before *b, p,* or *m:* せんべい *sembei,* "rice cracker."

As the use of syllabaries, rather than an alphabet, for Japanese indicates, much importance is attached to the syllables of the language. Whether represented in the Roman alphabet by one letter (the five vowels, the extra letter in double consonants, and the syllabic *n*), by two letters (e.g., *sa, no, ri*), or by three letters (e.g., *kya, shi, tsu*), each syllable has the same length and stress. A vowel should be put at the end of the syllable, the following consonant at the beginning of the next syllable; for example, *katsu,* "cutlet," is correctly pronounced *ka-tsu,* not *kat-su.*

CLOSED (on Mondays)	**CLOSED** TODAY	**CLOSING** TIME	**OPEN**	**IN PREPAR-** ATION
Teikyū-bi (*maishū getsuyōbi*)	*Honjitsu kyūgyō*	*Heiten jikoku*	*Eigyō-chū*	*Jumbi-chū*

Shop notices.

2 · FOOD MARKETS

Food markets in Japan generally fall into three categories: small shops selling predominantly one kind of food; supermarkets, where a variety of goods is sold; and convenience stores, which are open long hours and offer a limited selection of foods and supplies. Food markets are usually crowded toward the end of the afternoon, when local housewives do much of their daily shopping.

TYPES OF STORES

Neighborhood and Specialty Shops

Neighborhood shops are small stores that line a street called a *shōtengai* 商店街 "shop street." *Shōtengai* are found in just about any neighborhood and are where the local residents do much of their daily shopping. Each of the shops usually sells one type of item, such as meat, fish, or produce.

Specialty shops also usually sell one type of item, but look fancier than neighborhood shops and may offer such services as gift-boxing. Specialty shops may be found along *shōtengai,* but are not limited to these streets.

Most of these shops open at about 10 A.M. and close after dark, and many are closed on a certain day of the week, not necessarily Sunday. Shops close for up to a week during the New Year's holidays (beginning at the year end) and for several days during Obon, a Buddhist holiday which falls in mid-summer.

The words for some of the stores and the form in which they may appear on some signs are as follows:

魚屋	*sakana-ya*, fish market
肉屋	*niku-ya*, meat shop
鳥屋	*tori-ya*, poultry shop
果物屋	*kudamono-ya*, fruit store
八百屋	*yao-ya*, greengrocer's
パン屋	*pan-ya*, bakery
酒屋	*saka-ya*, liquor store
みそ屋	*miso-ya*, miso (fermented soybean paste) store
米屋	*kome-ya*, rice store
お茶屋	*ocha-ya*, tea store
豆腐屋	*tōfu-ya*, tofu (soybean curd) store

A shopkeeper is addressed and referred to by the word for the shop with the honorific -*san* added, for example, *nikuya-san*, "the butcher."

Other neighborhood and specialty shops include those which make and sell rice crackers *(sembei)*, candy and cookies, traditional tea sweets, and pickles *(tsukemono)*. There are also small grocery stores along many *shōtengai;* these carry a limited selection of the products found in a standard supermarket.

Prices in meat, fish, and fresh produce are often lower in neighborhood shops than in supermarkets. However, selection is sometimes more limited in the smaller shops. Freshness varies from store to store, but many items seem more consistently fresh in supermarkets.

Supermarkets

Supermarkets (スーパー *sūpā*) carry a variety of food and household items. They often have good fish and meat sections. Supermarkets vary in size from medium-sized stores to extensive markets covering several floors of a building. Some supermarkets associated with department-store chains sell appliances, kitchenware, and even bedding.

Supermarkets open at about 10 A.M. and close in the early evening. Some are open seven days a week, some are closed on a certain weekday, and some close at irregular intervals. Like neighborhood shops, most supermarkets close during the New Year's holidays and may close for several days during Obon.

Supermarkets may stock some imported products whose labels are written in the Roman alphabet and other writing systems. Imported items are found particularly on the shelves that display canned goods, cheese, coffee, jam, oil, sauces, soda, spices, and tea. Stores called "Western supermarkets" by foreign residents carry predominantly imported products, goods with labels written in the Roman alphabet, and Western cuts of meat.

Convenience Stores

Small markets called convenience stores carry a limited selection of basic food items and some take-out foods, such as ready-made sandwiches. Some of these stores are open 24 hours a day, 365 days a year, unlike neighborhood shops and supermarkets. Prices are often higher in convenience stores in order to compensate for the longer shopping hours.

SHOPPING PROCEDURE

Baskets that can be carried in the hand and/or pushcarts are placed at the entrance to many markets. Wet umbrellas are to be left in a rack at the door in some stores. At others, the umbrella is placed into a plastic bag provided by the store; you carry your bagged umbrella as you shop and dispose of the bag in a receptacle at the door as you leave.

At neighborhood shops, especially fish, meat, poultry, and produce markets, most items are displayed unwrapped.

Meat, chicken, and some fish items are sold by weight; you can buy any amount you like. Items of produce and some kinds of fish displayed on baskets the size of dinner plates or wrapped in clear plastic bags must be bought in the amount displayed. At supermarkets, on the other hand, most of the above items are sold prewrapped. Rolls of clear plastic bags that can be torn off one by one are placed above the fresh-food shelves in some supermarkets; these bags are to be used for an extra wrapping of individual meat, produce, tofu, and other perishable items.

At larger markets payment is made at check-out counters somewhere near the entrance. Occasionally, booths run by outside merchants sell special items within the store, and payment is expected at the booth itself. In some very large supermarkets, there may be separate cash registers for items like liquor and cigarettes. At small markets, the check-out counter may be placed wherever convenient, and an abacus or calculator may be used instead of a cash register.

The check-out clerk may put the items into white plastic bags with handles. At some stores, the customer is given the bags and has to pack the purchases, after payment is made, at a table slightly removed from the check-out counter. Small clear plastic bags for the separate wrapping of meat, produce, etc., may be given out by the clerk, or may be on rolls on the packing table. Paper bags are not used much, since they have become expensive to give out. The white plastic bags are capable of carrying great weights without tearing or breaking.

Home delivery is not usually provided by neighborhood food markets, unless you buy a large amount, live nearby, and are a regular customer. Department stores with food sections and Western supermarkets often provide delivery service. Sometimes a certain minimum amount must be purchased. Inquiry can be made by asking the clerk, *"Haitatsu shimasu ka?"* (Do you deliver?).

UNITS OF MEASUREMENT AND PRICE

The metric system is used for expressing the weight or volume of most products. Presenting weight in grams (g., グラム *guramu*) and kilograms (kg., キログラム *kirogura-mu*) instead of in ounces and pounds, and volume in millili-ters (ml., ミリリットル *miririttoru*) and liters (1., リットル *rittoru*) instead of in fluid ounces and quarts makes it diffi-cult at first to estimate quantities. The following indicates some equivalents between the two weight systems:

Pound / Ounces		Grams
$\frac{1}{4}$ lb. =	4 oz.	113 g.
$\frac{1}{2}$ =	8	227
$\frac{3}{4}$ =	12	340
1 =	16	454
2.2 =	35	1,000

One hundred grams is equivalent to $3\frac{1}{2}$ ounces, or slightly less than $\frac{1}{4}$ pound. For volume, 1 liter (1,000 ml.) can be considered equivalent to 1 quart (1 lit. = 1 qt. + $\frac{1}{4}$ cup). (See App. 2 for a fuller treatment of weights and measures.)

Prices are of course given in yen (円 or ¥, *en*). Prices for meat, fish, poultry and the like are most often expressed in yen per 100 grams (100 グラム当り *hyaku guramu atari*). The simultaneous conversion of two systems of units—currency and weight—may be a bit troublesome at first. Table 2 shows the conversion of yen per 100 grams to dollars per pound at several rates of exchange. The Table is based on

TABLE 2: Yen per 100 Grams to Dollars per Pound

¥/100 g.	¥/1b.	\$/1b. at the following exchange rates			
		¥150:\$1	¥160: \$1	¥175: \$1	¥200: \$1
¥50	¥227	\$1.51	\$1.42	\$1.30	\$1.14
100	454	3.03	2.84	2.59	2.27
150	681	4.54	4.26	3.89	3.40
200	908	6.05	5.68	5.19	4.54
250	1,135	7.57	7.09	6.49	5.67
300	1,362	9.08	8.51	7.78	6.81
400	1,816	12.11	11.35	10.38	9.08
500	2,270	15.13	14.19	12.97	11.35
600	2,724	18.16	17.03	15.57	13.62
700	3,178	21.19	19.86	18.16	15.89
800	3,632	24.21	22.70	20.75	18.16
900	4,086	27.24	25.54	23.35	20.43
1,000	4,540	30.27	28.38	25.94	22.70

the usual range of the exchange rate between yen and U.S. dollars but it can also be used to convert Canadian, Australian, and New Zealand dollars if the prevailing exchange rate falls within the range of the Table. If it does not, or if you are accustomed to another currency, divide the figure in the second column of the Table (¥/lb.) by the present exchange rate in terms of yen per unit of your currency. The answer is the price per pound in your currency. With experience, you will get used to prevailing prices and the yen-per-100-gram pricing method, and will no longer need to refer to other units.

As mentioned above, fresh fish and produce may be sold in set quantities, either by the piece or in groups. The following "units" are often seen on price signs next to the items. The price most often follows the unit, as shown in the example:

1コ/1ケ/1個*   *ikko,* a piece; each

EXAMPLE: 1コ 200円   *ikko 200 en,* 200 yen a piece

1本	*ippon,* 1 long item (e.g., a stalk of celery)
1列	*ichi-retsu,* 1 row (of fruit on a pallet)
1把	*ichi-wa,* 1 bunch (of spinach tied together)
1袋	*hito-fukuro,* one bag (of green peppers)
1舟	*hito-fune,* "1 boat," 1 long, flat tray (of squid, shrimp, etc.)
1切	*hito-kire,* 1 slice (of fish or meat)
1盛	*hito-mori,* 1 pile (of several fresh fish on a plate)
1パック	*hito-pakku,* 1 pack (of strawberries)
1皿	*hito-sara,* 1 plate (of fresh clams)
1束	*hito-taba* (synonymous with *ichi-wa,* above)
1山	*hito-yama,* "1 mountain"; 1 pile (of oranges on a container)

Some additional points concerning pricing methods are as follows:

· Unit prices, such as the cost per 100 grams, are not always displayed with a product. It is necessary to determine the most economic brand item by item.

· The price of a larger container of a given product is not necessarily any cheaper, in terms of unit price, than a smaller container of the same item. The unit price may be the same for all sizes of the same product; on occasion, the unit price of the larger size has actually been found to be higher.

---

* The numeral 1 may be replaced by the character 一 "one" in many of these examples. Any numeral, of course, may precede the unit, e.g., 2コ, 3本, etc. See Appendix 1 for an explanation of the pronunciation of numbers and units.

· Goods are usually not reduced in price if two or three of the same item are purchased.

· If a store runs a sale on a product, the sale price may be marked on the product only at a special display, while the same product at its usual spot on the shelves will continue to carry the regular, not the sale, price.

· A product on special sale is not necessarily old stock. It may in fact be newer than the same, non-sale, product at its usual spot on the shelves.

· To clear their stock, some stores suddenly reduce prices on fresh items shortly before closing time.

· Some common words denoting special sales, found on signs in front of shops and on shelves, are 特価 *tokka,* "sale price"; 特売品 *tokubaihin,* "sale items"; セール *sēru,* "sale"; バーゲン *bāgen,* "bargain"; and 大売出し *ōuridashi* "big sale."

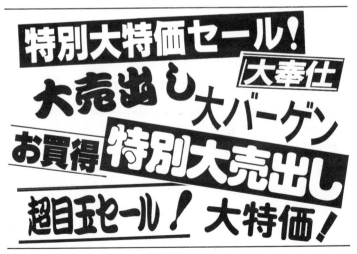

Ads and signs for special sales.

3 · HOW TO READ A FOOD LABEL

For the person who does not read Japanese, labels may seem at first to be a confusing arrangement of symbols, none of which give a clue to the contents of the package. One does not know whether the largest characters represent the brand name, the manufacturer's name, or the generic name of the product. Even if a person is vaguely familiar with kana and knows that the largest writing on the label is in these symbols, the elaborate and decorative form in which they appear may make them difficult to read.

Labels on Japanese foods and household goods contain a wealth of information, sometimes far more than appears on labels elsewhere in the world. The aim of this chapter is to provide those who do not read Japanese with the information necessary to understand a label.

PRICE LABELS

Preprinted labels on fresh meat, fish, produce, and prepared foods that have been wrapped in the store usually contain the following information:

加工年月日	*kakō nengappi*, date of packaging
100 g 当り (円)	*hyaku guramu atari (en)*, price per 100 grams (in yen)
正味量	*shōmiryō*, net weight
値段 or 価格	*nedan* or *kakaku*, price

The date is expressed in the order year 年, month 月, day 日. The year is usually given in terms of the era-name and year of reign of the current emperor. The year 1985 is Shōwa 60; 1986 is Shōwa 61 (written "昭和 61," "S. 61," or simply "61"); and so on. A date rendered "S. 61.2.3" thus means February 3, 1986. When a new emperor begins to reign, the era-name is changed and the years start over again at 1.

The small price sticker on most other items may have a number to the left of the price, for example, 3 ¥138. The 3 does not mean "3 for 138 yen," but is a code for the cashier.

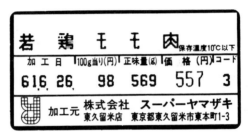

Label for packaged fresh chicken.

PRICE STICKERS

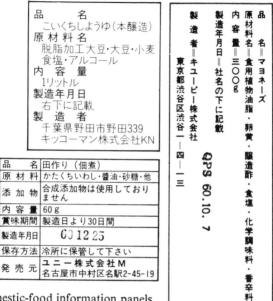

品　　　名
　こいくちしょうゆ（本醸造）
原材料名
　脱脂加工大豆・大豆・小麦
　食塩・アルコール
内　容　量
　1リットル
製造年月日
　右下に記載
製　造　者
　千葉県野田市野田339
　キッコーマン株式会社KN

品　　　名	田作り（佃煮）
原　材　料	かたくちいわし・醬油・砂糖・他
添　加　物	合成添加物は使用しておりません
内　容　量	60 g
賞味期間	製造日より30日間
製造年月日	60 12 25
保存方法	冷所に保管して下さい
発　売　元	ユニー株式会社M 名古屋市中村区名駅2-45-19

品　　名‖マヨネーズ
原材料名‖食用植物油脂・卵黄・醸造酢・食塩・化学調味料・香辛料
内　容　量‖300g
製造年月日‖社名の下に記載

QPS 60.10.7

製　造　者‖キューピー株式会社
東京都渋谷区渋谷一―四―一三

Domestic-food information panels.

PACKAGE LABELS

The Information Panel

To get the important information from a label, it is necessary to go to the back of the bottle, box, or package. On all food packages in Japan, with the exception of those containing tea, seaweed, and some noodles, the back label carries an information panel usually, but not always, separated from the rest of the writing by a border. While the lettering of the front label may be decorative, the printing of the information in the panel looks very much like the printing of the kanji and kana in this book.

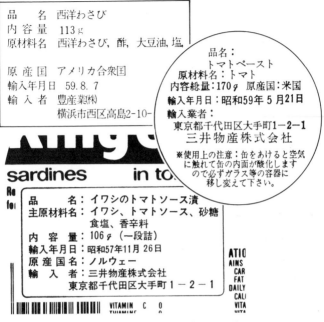

品　　名　西洋わさび
内 容 量　113ℊ
原材料名　西洋わさび，酢，大豆油，塩，

原 産 国　アメリカ合衆国
輸入年月日　59. 8. 7
輸 入 者　豊産業㈱
　　　　　横浜市西区高島2-10-

品名：
トマトペースト
原材料名：トマト
内容総量：170ℊ 原産国：米国
輸入年月日：昭和59年 5 月21日
輸入業者：
東京都千代田区大手町1－2－1
三井物産株式会社
※使用上の注意：缶をあけると空気
に触れて缶の内面が酸化します
ので必ずガラス等の容器に
移し変えて下さい。

sardines　in to

品　　名：イワシのトマトソース漬
主原材料名：イワシ，トマトソース，砂糖
　　　　　　食塩，香辛料
内 容 量：106ℊ （一段詰）
輸入年月日：昭和57年11月26日
原 産 国 名：ノルウェー
輸 入 者：三井物産株式会社
　　　　　　東京都千代田区大手町 1 － 2 － 1

VITAMIN　C　0

Imported-food information panels.

For foods imported from abroad, the information panel (in Japanese) may be part of the label itself, as with domestic products, or it may be on a separate sticker attached to the package (sometimes, unfortunately, covering the original information panel in the foreign language).

The words in the information panel are usually written horizontally, left to right. Sometimes, however, the panel is presented vertically, so that reading proceeds down each column starting with the column furthest to the right. This presentation occurs more rarely, usually on packages that are long and narrow, such as those for wrapping noodles.

品　　名　　冷凍食品ニンニクの芽	凍結前加熱の有無　加熱してありません
原 材 料 名　　ニンニクの芽	加熱調理の必要性　加熱してください
内　容　量　　250グラム	原産国　中華人民共和国
製造年月日　　枠外の裏面に記載してあります	販売者　日魯漁業株式会社 NGK151
保 存 方 法　　−18℃以下で保存して下さい	東京都千代田区有楽町1-12-1
使 用 方 法　　枠外の裏面に記載してあります	

The following are the main categories in the information panel (some categories may be missing from some information panels but may appear elsewhere on the product):

品名	*himmei*, product name
原材料名	*genzairyōmei*, ingredients
内容量	*naiyōryō*, net weight or volume
製造年月日	*seizō nengappi*, date of manufacture
⌈保存方法	*hozon hōhō*, storage information
⌊保存上の注意	*hozonjō no chūi*
⌈調理方法	*chōri hōhō*, method of preparation
⌊作り方	*tsukuri-kata*, cooking instructions
⌈賞味期限	*shōmi kigen*, "to be eaten by this date"
⌊賞味期日	*shōmi kijitsu*
製造者*	*seizōsha*, manufacturer
販売者	*hambaisha*, seller

Preservation Hozon (handwritten annotation in left margin)

Additional categories appear on the labels of imported goods:

原産国名	*gensankokumei*, country of origin
輸入年月日	*yunyū nengappi*, date of import
輸入業者	*yunyūgyōsha*, importer
発売元	*hatsubai-moto*, distributor

　* The character 元 *moto* may replace 者 *sha* in some cases with no change in meaning.

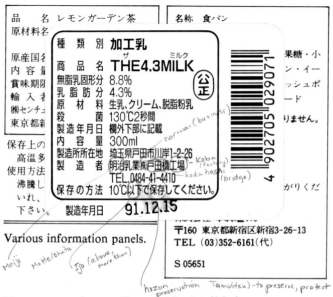

品　名	レモンガーデン茶
原材料名	

種 類 別	加工乳
商 品 名	THE4.3MILK
無脂乳固形分	8.8%
乳 脂 肪 分	4.3%
原 材 料	生乳、クリーム、脱脂粉乳
殺 菌	130℃2秒間
製 造 年 月 日	欄外下部に記載
内 容 量	300ml
製 造 所 在 地	埼玉県戸田市川岸1-2-26
製 造 者	明治乳業㈱戸田橋工場
	TEL.0484-41-4410
保 存 の 方 法	10℃以下で保存してください。

製造年月日　91.12.15

名称　食パン

〒160　東京都新宿区新宿3-26-13
TEL　(03)352-6161(代)

S 05651

Various information panels.

These categories are discussed in detail below.

品名 *himmei* product name

The name of the product in the information panel is the generic name of the item, not the brand or manufacturer's name. The readings of the characters for many names can be determined by comparing the name printed in the appropriate chapter of Part II of this book. (For instance, for a bottle of liquid that might be a detergent, the characters in the information panel to the right of *himmei* can be compared with the characters in the "dish detergent" section of Chap. 19.)

The term 名称 *meishō* appears on some products in addition to *himmei* as an even more general identification of the product.

品 名	マーガリン
原 材 料 名	コーン油、脱脂粉乳、食塩、 レシチン、トコフェロール、 乳化剤、着香料、ビタミンA油、 β-カロチン
内 容 量	225g
製 造 年 月 日	側面に記載
保 存 方 法	10℃以下で保存してください。
販 売 者	明治乳業株式会社 OF 東京都中央区京橋2-3-6

Information panel (second line lists ingredients).

原材料名 *genzairyōmei* ingredients

The ingredients listed on a label are listed in the order of their magnitude in the product, from greatest to least. The words for the ingredients are separated by a comma, a raised dot, or a space. Information in the appropriate chapter of Part II and the Vocabulary List (p. 165) will be helpful in deciphering the ingredients of a product.

Japanese law is strict about food additives, so ingredients of domestically produced products are usually derived from natural foods. Listed below are a few common ingredients that may be of concern. The artificial ingredients included in this list usually appear only on labels of imported foods; the last three items are common in domestic foods as well as imported.

合成着色料	*gōsei chakushokuryō*, artificial color*
着香料	*chakkōryō*, artificial flavoring
合成保存料	*gōsei hozonryō*, artificial preservative
合成甘味料	*gōsei kammiryō*, artificial sweetener
化学調味料	*kagaku chōmiryō*, monosodium glutamate (msg.)

* Japanese does not distinguish between singular and plural. Therefore, when, for example, *gōsei chakushokuryō* appears on a label, one or more artificial flavorings may be in the product.

塩 or 食塩   *shio* or *shokuen*, salt
砂糖   *satō*, sugar

The prefix 合成 *gōsei* means "synthetic." The prefix for "natural" is 天然 *tennen*. The suffix 使用 *shiyō*, which may appear after some of the above words, means "[has been] used."

内容量 *naiyōryō* net weight or volume
    The third category in the information panel is usually the net weight, listed in grams or kilograms, or the net volume, listed in milliliters or liters. Other "units," for example, 4人分 (4 *nimbun*) "serves 4 people," may be given after the weight or volume (see p. 38 for a list of similar terms).

製造年月日 *seizō nengappi* date of manufacture
    The date of production will be printed in the order year–month–day. The year designates the year of the current emperor's reign (see p. 29). If no date appears next to this category in the information panel, there will be instructions to look elsewhere on the label, where the date will be stamped in ink.

保存方法 *hozon hōhō* storage information
保存上の注意 *hozonjō no chūi*
    Storage information, if it appears on a label, is sometimes placed below the "date of manufacture" line, but it often appears outside the information panel, sometimes in a color different from the other writing on the label. Terms similar to *hozon hōhō* are 取り扱い上の注意 *tori-atsukaijō no chūi*, "method of handling" and 使用上の注意 *shiyōjō no chūi*, "care/caution in use."
    Temperature information is given in degrees centigrade

(°C). A temperature of 5°C to 10°C refers to refrigeration; 0°C is the freezing point. (See App. 2, p. 151, for centigrade–Fahrenheit conversion tables.) The best storage practice is to store the product at home as it is stored in the market (except for eggs, which are not refrigerated in stores), and to keep opened containers of jam, mayonnaise, and the like in the refrigerator.

調理方法 *chōri hōhō* method of preparation
作り方 *tsukuri-kata* cooking instructions

If the method of preparation of the product is simple, a brief description is given in the information panel. Other terms seen are 使用方法 *shiyō hōhō,* "method of use," and 召し上り方 *meshiagari-kata,* "method of preparation." In most cases, however, the user is referred to another part of the label, where the instructions are stated in detail. (See App. 3, p. 152, for terms used in cooking instructions.)

賞味期限 *shōmi kigen* "to be eaten by this date"
賞味期日 *shōmi kijitsu*

The date by which the product should be consumed appears on the labels of some perishable items, either in the information panel or stamped elsewhere on the label. Look for a date and see if the above kanji precede it; if they do not, the date is probably the date of manufacture. A term similar to the above is 賞味期間 *shōmi kikan,* which refers to the period (usually in days, 日) from the date of manufacture in which the product may be used.

製造者 *seizōsha* manufacturer
販売者 *hambaisha* seller

The manufacturer's or seller's name and address is printed on the last line of the panel.

原産国名 *gensankokumei* country of origin

Although the names of a few countries are written in kanji, most are written in katakana; pronunciations of the names are usually based on the English word for the country. In addition, front labels usually bear the name of the country in English. Two common kanji names are 中華人民共和国 *Chūka Jimmin Kyōwakoku* (or 中国 *Chūgoku*), the People's Republic of China; and 中華民国・台湾省 *Chūka Minkoku, Taiwan-shō,* the Republic of China (Taiwan). Some products imported from Hong Kong 香港, bearing these kanji on the front label, may have the characters for the People's Republic of China in the information panel.

輸入年月日 *yunyū nengappi* date of import

For most imported items, the date of import rather than the date of manufacture appears in the information panel. It may therefore be impossible to tell how old the product really is, although an estimation can be made if several months shipping and handling time are allowed for.

輸入業者 *yunyūgyōsha* importer
発売元 *hatsubai-moto* distributor

The importer's name and address, rather than the manufacturer's, is given at the bottom of the label on imported items. If the importer does not actually distribute the product, the distributor's name is given also.

Certain items of information appear less frequently in the information panel. These include method of pasteurization or sterilization, information about the inspection of the product, specific uses of the product (主な用途 *omo na yōto*), and additives (添加物 *tenkabutsu*).

Front-label information.

The Front Label

As mentioned above, the user is often referred to parts of the label outside the information panel for date, storage, and preparation information. A few other helpful items of information appear on food labels, usually on the front and/or sides of the package. Some of these are as follows:

無添加	*mutenka,* no additives
無農薬栽培	*munōyaku saibai,* no agricultural chemicals
即席	*sokuseki,* instant
x 袋入	~*fukuro-iri, x* packets enclosed
x 個入/コ入	~*ko-iri, x* number of portions
x 人分	~*nimbun, x* number of people/servings
x 人前	~*nimmae*
x 皿分	~*sarabun*

The last five items above are preceded by a number (represented here by *x*). Individual servings may be smaller than what your family is used to.

The letters JAS (Japan Agricultural Standard) surrounded by an incomplete circle appear on many front labels. This symbol is a kind of seal of approval testifying to the quality and safety of the product.

PART III

FOODS AND

HOUSEHOLD NEEDS

The chapters in this part contain descriptions of most basic foods and many household needs: what these items look like, where they can be found in the market, how they are different from Western products, what their names are in Japanese, how these names appear in kanji or kana, when they are in season if appropriate, and, in some cases, how to use the product.

The entry for a particular item is presented in the following order: the English word, the kanji and/or kana, and the romanization of the Japanese term in italics. A sample heading follows:

Peaches	桃/もも	*momo*
↑	↑ ↑	↑
English word	kanji kana	romanization

Items within each section of a chapter are arranged alphabetically according to their names in English, except when there is no common English word for the product, in which case the romanized Japanese word is inserted into the alphabetical sequence.

When a generic name or other term made up of two (or more) words in the original language (e.g., "baking powder") is borrowed into Japanese, the term may appear on labels as one long word in katakana, rather than as two separate words. In the entries and text of this book, however, such terms are shown with a space between their constituents, for ease in reading.

Brand names are listed in the form written on the label, with a romanized transcription for kanji and kana brand-names. If a brand name is rendered in this book in Roman letters only, that is the form in which it appears on the label. The mention of a particular brand does not constitute an endorsement.

No-brand (無印 *mujirushi*) products, sold at prices below those of name-brand products, come in plain packages and are sometimes displayed together in a separate area of the store, rather than distributed product by product on the shelves where name brands are displayed. There are also special stores which deal only in no-brand products.

If you can't find a particular product at a market, you can point out to a clerk the word for the product in this book and ask, *"Kore wa doko desu ka?"* (Where is this?).

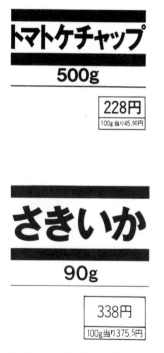

品名●トマトケチャップ
原材料名● トマト、糖類(砂糖、ぶどう糖 果糖液糖)、醸造酢、食塩、玉ねぎ 香辛料
内容量●500g
製造年月日●枠外上部に記載
販売者● 株式会社 江原産業EK26 〒170 東京都豊島区 東池袋3-1-1

賞味期間　製造日より1年間

合成・天然着色料、合成甘味料、合成
保存料はいっさい使用しておりません。

品名	さきいか
内容量	90g
製造年月日	欄外に記載
賞味期間	製造年月日より3ヶ月
添加物	合成保存料使用
販売者	株式会社 江原産業　EN04 〒170東京都豊島区東池袋3-1-1

●保存方法　直射日光、高温多湿の場所をさけ、
開封後はお早目にお召し上がりください。

Labels and information panels for no-brand products.

4 · BAKING NEEDS AND SPICES

Baking needs are not always placed together in a market. Yeast and baking powder will probably be near one another, while extracts may be in a separate part of the store and spices in another. (In this book, flour is described in Chap. 8, and salt and sugar in Chap. 15.)

Baking powder ベーキング パウダー *bēkingu paudā*. Baking powder comes in small cans and is found near the yeast or flour. The generic name often appears in English on the label.

Baking soda (bicarbonate of soda) ベーキング ソーダ *bēkingu sōda* or 炭酸水素ナトリウム *tansan suiso natoryūmu* or 重曹 *jūsō*. Baking soda is not always sold in food markets. When it is, it usually comes in small plastic packets. It is often available in drugstores under the second name above or the abbreviation *tansan*.

Chocolate (baking) チョコレート *chokorēto*. If it is available, baking chocolate (usually Hershey's) is found near other baking items or near the candies. If it cannot be found, 3 teaspoons of cocoa and 1 tablespoon of shortening can be substituted for 1 ounce (28 g.) of baking chocolate.

Chocolate chips チョコレート チップス *chokorēto chippusu*. Domestic and imported (Hershey's, Nestlé's) brands of chocolate chips are available, either with other baking needs or near the candies. The chips are usually visible through the clear plastic of the package.

Cocoa ココア *kokoa*. Cocoa comes in cans the size of the well-known Hershey can and in boxes. Sweetened cocoa, usually for drinking, has the word, 砂糖 *satō* "sugar," written in the list of ingredients.

Extracts エッセンス *essensu*. McCormick's and My are the most prevalent brands of extracts available. They come in the usual small bottles. The following is a list of some of the names as they may appear on front labels:

アーモンド オイル	*āmondo oiru*, almond oil
バナナ	*banana*, banana
レモン	*remon*, lemon
メロン	*meron*, melon
オレンジ	*orenji*, orange
パイナップル	*painappuru*, pineapple
ストロベリー	*sutoroberii*, strawberry
バニラ	*banira*, vanilla

Gelatin ゼラチン *zerachin*. Unflavored gelatin is usually stocked with the flavored dessert gelatins, not with other baking needs. It comes in two forms: leaf (リーフ *riifu*) and powdered (パウダー *paudā*). Leaf gelatin comes in clear plastic packages, five leaves to a package. The leaves are about 6 by 18 centimeters (2½ by 7 in.), have a diamond-shaped grid printed on them, and are slightly tinted. Powdered gelatin comes in 5-gram ($\frac{1}{5}$ oz). packets, several packets to a box. (See App. 4, p. 154, for instructions for using both kinds of gelatin.)

Spices 香辛料 *kōshinryō*. Spices used in Western foods are sold in the usual small glass jars bearing labels in English. Some spices, such as bay leaves (laurel), are also sold in small flat plastic bags. When containers bear only Japanese writing, the contents are most likely pepper (コショウ *koshō*), curry (カレー *karē*), or one of a number of spices used in traditional Japanese cooking. Ginger (しょうが *shōga*) and garlic (ガーリック *gārikku*) are also common on both the Japanese and Western spice shelves. The kanji 粉 (before a word, *kona;* after a word, *ko*) means "powdered" or "finely ground." Other prefixes are あらびき *arabiki,* "coarsely ground," and 粒 *tsubu,* "whole" (as for pepper corns).

In addition to the above, the following are the most common Japanese dry or powdered condiments that may not bear English labels. These items are found in spice jars, small cans, and plastic bags. Many of the names are preceded or followed by 粉 (powdered).

(一味)唐辛子/ とうがらし	*(ichimi) tōgarashi,* cayenne pepper
七味とうがらし	*shichimi tōgarashi* (a hot mixture of seven spices, including cayenne pepper)
わさび	*wasabi,* Japanese horseradish (see also p. 100)
からし	*karashi,* Japanese mustard
塩コショウ	*shio koshō,* salt-and-pepper mixture
山椒/さんしょう	*sanshō* (a seasoning made from the pod of the prickly ash)
胡麻/ごま	*goma,* sesame seeds
黒ごましお	*kurogoma-shio,* black sesame seeds and salt

Yeast (dry) ドライイースト *dorai iisuto.* Dry yeast comes in small cans and boxes. Two teaspoons of dry yeast equal 1 packet of yeast as sold in the West.

5 · BREAD, CEREAL, AND PASTA

Bread

Although there has not been a long tradition in Japan of baking and eating bread (パン *pan*), a large variety of fresh bread is available daily at supermarkets and bakeries. Croissants, dinner rolls, and Italian and French breads are easily found, as are white breads of cake-like consistency and raisin bread. Whole wheat, rye, and dark breads may be harder to find.

Some larger supermarkets have bakeries on the premises, and bread is sold still hot from the oven. When sold in packages, bread is either sliced or whole. The thickness of slices varies, but can be seen through the clear plastic of the package.

Many stores carry English muffins, which are wrapped in clear plastic, four to a package. Plain, whole wheat, raisin, corn, cheese, and seaweed English muffins are sold. These words are written in English on the package.

Probably the most troublesome bread for a newcomer is the hamburger roll. The Japanese put bean jam (あん *an*) in surprising places, including a roll that looks as if it were made for hamburgers. Bean jam is dark reddish brown and sweet and has the texture of Mexican refried beans. When buying hamburger rolls, select round rolls no more than $3\frac{1}{2}$ centimeters ($1\frac{1}{2}$ in.) thick, and avoid ones that feel heavy and that have poppy seeds on the top. When in doubt, ask a sales clerk, *"An ga haitte-imasu ka?"* (Do these have bean jam in them?). Bean jam also comes in some doughnuts (あんドーナツ *an dōnatsu*).

AN-PAN
(bean-jam buns)

Pepperidge Farm bread stuffing is often sold in Western and other supermarkets, particularly in the autumn. Don't wait until the last minute to buy it, or it may not be available.

Breakfast Cereal

Breakfast cereals are sold at most markets, although the variety at smaller markets is often limited. Domestically produced cold cereals include several Kellogg's products, all with names printed in English somewhere on the package. Imported cold cereals are all labeled in the Roman alphabet. Photographs of package contents are found on most products.

Domestic and imported brands of oatmeal are found in most supermarkets. All labels have the word "oatmeal" in English. Cooking times vary considerably, so instructions should be consulted. If the cooking time is more than five minutes, the oatmeal should be prepared in a double boiler. Other kinds of hot cereal are not commonly found.

Western supermarkets usually carry the most extensive selections of breakfast cereals, but because of import delays, some varieties may be out of stock for months before returning to the shelves.

Pasta

Spaghetti, macaroni, Western noodles, and other pasta can be found in large supermarkets. Most products are imported from Italy or the United States. See-through packages or pictures eliminate any need to guess the contents. When the Japanese import label is pasted directly over the cooking instructions on the package, cooking time can be determined by referring to the information on the import label; look for a number followed by the kanji 分 *fun,* "minutes."

Bakery sign *(left)* in a local shōtengai.

6 · DAIRY PRODUCTS AND MARGARINE

Dairy products and margarine are usually sold near one another in refrigerated cases in food markets. Their packages are similar to those of corresponding products found in the West. Some of the categories in the information panel of dairy-product labels are different from those on other products (see Chap. 3): 種類別 *shuruibetsu,* "classification," replaces 品名 *himmei;* 使用原料 *shiyō genryō,* 原料名 *genryōmei,* or 主要混合物 *shuyōkongōbutsu* (all mean essentially "ingredients") replaces 原材料名 *genzairyōmei.* A line with the heading 成分 *seibun,* "composition," lists the percentages of such components as butterfat.

Butter バター *batā*

Butter is usually packaged in blocks of 200 or 225 grams (7 or 8 oz.). Butter is not found in stick form, but a 225-gram block cut in half yields 2 quarter-pound sticks. The major brands of butter come in yellow boxes with the word バター displayed in prominent characters. (A product in a lighter yellow box with a scene of black-and-white cows in a pasture can easily be mistaken for butter. This is actually Snow Brand Cheese; this name appears on the side, but not the top, of the box.)

Unsalted butter is packaged in boxes similar to those of regular butter. Look for the characters 無塩 *muen,* "salt free," printed in a prominent place on the label.

Cheese チーズ *chiizu*

A wide variety of imported natural cheese is available

in some large supermarkets and most department stores that have food sections. Sticks, singly and in cardboard cylinders, and blocks of smoked cheese (スモーク チーズ *sumōku chiizu*) are also seen. The average food market, however, has mostly processed cheese (プロセス チーズ *purosesu chiizu*) on the shelves.

Processed cheese comes in three main forms: rectangular blocks, individually wrapped slices, and small wedges and blocks wrapped in foil. With the exception of American-style processed cheese, Japanese-made cheeses often taste very different from their Western counterparts.

A product called Fresh Cheese is sold in a container like that used for cottage cheese. This product has the consistency of thick yogurt, but not the tartness.

Cottage Cheese カッテージ チーズ *kattēji chiizu*

Cottage cheese comes in tubs similar to those found in the West. Japanese cottage cheese crumbles easily. It can be used successfully in lasagne as a substitute for ricotta, although it is drier than ricotta.

Cream クリーム *kuriimu*

Cream is available in cans, often found near the coffee. The word クリーム is written prominently on the can.

Liquid coffee creamer comes in small brown jugs and in small individual servings contained in plastic bags. These are found refrigerated near the dairy products or unrefrigerated near the coffee. Liquid creamer may or may not contain dairy products; common ingredients are non-fat milk solids (無脂乳固形 *mushinyūkokei*) and either vegetable oil (植物油 *shokubutsuyu*) or cream.

Powdered creamer, in jars and in packages of individual servings, is stored near the coffee. Coffeemate and Creap are common brands. Powdered creamer may or may not contain dairy products; corn syrup (コーン シロップ *kōn shiroppu*) and casein (カゼイン *kazein*) are found in several brands.

Cream Cheese クリーム チーズ *kuriimu chiizu*

Cream cheese is readily available in most food stores under a variety of brand names; Philadelphia Brand and Kiri are the most prevalent. Philadelphia Brand is made in Australia and seems to be harder to spread than the American-made counterpart.

A box of cheese in the dairy case that says "creamy cheese" is a soft type of cheese, not cream cheese.

Ice Cream アイス クリーム *aisu kuriimu*

An assortment of imported and domestic ice cream and other frozen dairy products can be found at most supermarkets. Imported brands have labels in the Roman alphabet. The labels of domestic brands are usually written in Japanese. On domestic brands the name of the flavor often appears within parentheses or a circle. The most common flavors are as follows:

チョコレート	*chokorēto*, chocolate
コーヒー	*kōhii*, coffee
桃/もも or ピーチ	*momo* or *piichi*, peach
いちご or ストロベリー	*ichigo* or *sutoroberii*, strawberry
バニラ	*banira*, vanilla

Margarine マーガリン *māgarin*

With the exception of cooking margarines (料理用の マーガリン *ryōri-yō no māgarin*), most margarine is sold in 225-gram (8-oz.) and/or 450-gram (1-1b.) tubs rather than in stick form. Ingredients from one brand to another are remarkably similar, but the kind of vegetable oil or oils varies. The information panel usually gives only the Japanese word for "vegetable oil"; the word(s) for the specific oil or oils may appear in the promotional writing elsewhere on the package, although some brands leave the type of vegetable oil unspecified. Some cooking margarines contain animal fat in addition to vegetable oil, as seen in Table 3.

The ingredients most commonly found in margarine are listed below in approximately the order in which they appear in the information panel:

植物油	*shokubutsuyu,** vegetable oil
動物油脂	*dōbutsu-yushi*, animal fat
脱脂粉乳	*dasshi-funnyū*, non-fat milk powder
塩 or 食塩	*shio* or *shokuen*, salt
乳化剤	*nyūkazai*, emulsifier
香料	*kōryō*, flavorings
β-カロチン	*beta-karochin*, beta-carotene (a natural coloring)

The following are the names of the most common oils used (each is followed by the character 油):

コーン or とうもろこし	*kōn* or *tōmorokoshi*, corn
パーム	*pāmu*, palm
紅花 or サフラワー	*benibana* or *safurawā*, safflower
大豆	*daizu*, soybean
向日葵/ひまわり or サンフラワー	*himawari* or *sanfurawā*, sunflower

* The character 油, "oil," as a suffix may sometimes be pronounced *abura* as well as *yu*.

TABLE 3: Ingredients in Common Brands of Margarine

Brand Name	Oil(s)	Other
Cooking:		
Borden クッキング (cooking)	Vegetable; animal fat	New milk yeast; 450-g. package only
Rama ケーキ (cake)	Soy; palm	"Low" salt; no milk ingredient
雪印ケーキ (Snow Brand cake)	Vegetable	No salt
雪印 S (Snow Brand S)	Vegetable; animal fat	450-g. package only
General Use:		
Benibana	Safflower	Annato and β-carotene colors
Borden コーン 100 (Corn 100)	Corn	——
Corn Marina	Corn	Non-fat milk solids
Hotel	Safflower	Fermented milk; soybean lecithin; natural plant and annato colors; no flavoring or β-carotene
Koiwai	Vegetable	Milk curds
Marina White	Vegetable	——
Rama ヘルス (health)	Safflower; palm sunflower	Vitamins E and A; tocopherol
Rama ソフト (soft)	Soy; palm	Vitamin A
Rama スティック (stick)	Soy; palm	Vitamin A
Snow Brand Neo Margarine	Soy; palm	——
Snow Brand ネオソフト (neo-soft)	Soy; corn	——
雪印サフラワー (Snow Brand safflower)	Safflower	——

Note: Unless stated under "Other," all margarines contain non-fat milk powder (or, if stated, another "milk" ingredient), salt, emulsifier, flavorings, and beta-carotene.

Except as noted, margarine is sold in 225-gram packages. (Some brands are sold in both 225-gram and 450-gram packages.)

An additional term seen on margarine labels is リノール酸 60%, *rinōrusan* 60%, "60 percent linoleic acid" (among the fatty acids making up the oil). Linoleic acid is an essential fatty acid helpful in reducing levels of blood cholesterol.

Several brands of margarine-butter mixtures exist. These products do not have information panels on their labels. Most of these mixtures contain some combination of the ingredients listed above plus butter or butterfat (乳脂肪 *nyūshibō*). The butterfat content ranges from 4 to 20 percent.

Milk 牛乳 *gyūnyū*

There are three basic types of fresh milk available. All are sold in 1-liter (1-qt.) containers of the usual shape. Regular milk is called *gyūnyū* 牛乳 "milk"; this word appears on the *shuruibetsu* 種類別 line of the information panel and on the front label, where the word "milk" often appears as well. Regular milk contains no additives and is usually homogenized. (The front label of some brands of regular milk bear in large writing the characters 成分無調整 *seibun muchōsei,* which means that nothing has been added to the milk.)

The second type is called *kakōnyū* 加工乳 "processed milk"; the most common form of processed milk is *rōfatto* ローファット "low fat." The former word appears both in the information panel and on the front label, while ローファット appears on the front label only. Processed milk contains milk and other milk products, such as non-fat milk powder, non-fat condensed milk, and cream; it does not contain any non-milk additives. Brands vary in the kind and number of milk products added. "Low fat" varieties of processed milk are characterized by a reduction in butterfat content as well as the addition of non-fat milk products.

The third kind of milk is called *nyūinryō* 乳飲料 "milk beverage." Like processed milk, brands of milk beverage may contain additional milk products and a reduced percentage of butterfat, but their primary characteristic is that they contain non-milk additives such as vitamins.

An ultra-pasteurized long-life milk is packaged in 1-liter containers with all eight corners square; the carton is shorter than ordinary ones. This type of milk does not come in low-fat or milk-beverage form. The most common brand is Kagome. Various types of plain and flavored milks, as well as soybean milk (豆乳 *tōnyū*), are sold in smaller containers, to be used mostly as snack drinks.

Not one of the brands of milk I have examined has vitamin D added, although some brands contain other vitamins (ビタミン *bitamin*) such as riboflavin and vitamins C and E. Vitamin D is essential for the absorption of calcium. It is not abundant in natural foods, but it can be produced in the body when the skin comes in contact with the ultraviolet rays of the sun. Clouds and air pollution interfere with ultraviolet rays. If either condition exists for extended periods of time where you live, vitamin D may be a concern, especially for young children.

Information about percentages of butterfat (乳脂肪分 *nyūshibō-bun*) and of non-fat milk solids (無脂乳固形分 *mushinyū-kokei-bun*) is usually available on the *seibun* 成分 line of the information panel. The butterfat content of regular milk is generally between 3.5 and 4 percent; some milk may have a higher butterfat content. Low-fat milk contains about 1.5 percent butterfat. The butterfat content of milk-beverage products ranges from 0 percent for a brand called "Non Fat" to about the percentage found in regular milk. The higher the butterfat content, the lower the proportion of non-fat milk solids. Since calcium and protein are contained in non-fat milk solids, milk with a high butterfat content contains less calcium and protein.

Condensed milk コンデンス ミルク *kondensu miruku* is sold in cans. All brands seem to be sweetened. Percentages of sugar (砂糖 *satō*), non-fat milk solids, and butterfat are listed on the can.

Evaporated milk エバミルク *ebamiruku* is available in cans. No sugar is added. The percentages of non-fat milk solids and butterfat are listed on the can.

Powdered whole milk 全脂粉乳 *zenshi-funnyū* is found in some stores, where it is placed near the coffee on the shelves. The percentage of butterfat is given on the label.

Skim milk スキム ミルク *sukimu miruku* is available in powdered form, in cardboard cartons and in cans, stored near the coffee. The katakana above appear prominently on the front label, but not in the information panel. The proportion of butterfat in skim milk is usually 1 percent or below; the exact amount appears on the label. Liquid skim milk that contains no additives is not available as of this writing.

Sour Cream サワー クリーム *sawā kuriimu*
The front labels of sour cream usually carry the name in both English and katakana. This product is thick and dense. The addition of yogurt will make the consistency thinner without affecting the flavor.

Yogurt ヨーグルト *yōguruto*
Yogurt for eating and yogurt for drinking are both sold;

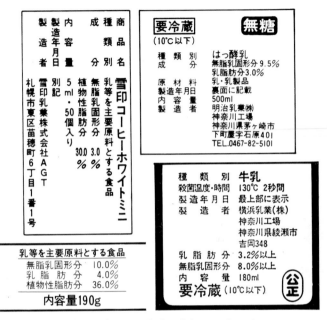

要冷蔵
（10℃以下）

無糖

商　品　名	雪印コーヒーホワイトミニ
種　類　別	乳等を主要原料とする食品
成　分	無脂乳固形分 3.0％ 植物性脂肪分 30.0％
内　容　量	5 ml・50個入り
製造年月日	別記
製　造　者	雪印乳業株式会社AGT 札幌市東区苗穂町6丁目1番1号

種　類　別	はっ酵乳
成　分	無脂乳固形分 9.5％ 乳脂肪分 3.0％
原　材　料	乳・乳製品
製造年月日	裏面に記載
内　容　量	500ml
製　造　者	明治乳業㈱ 神奈川工場 神奈川県茅ヶ崎市 下町屋字石原401 TEL.0467-82-5101

乳等を主要原料とする食品

無脂乳固形分	10.0％
乳　脂　肪　分	4.0％
植物性脂肪分	36.0％

内容量190g

種　類　別	牛乳
殺菌温度・時間	130℃ 2秒間
製造年月日	最上部に表示
製　造　者	横浜乳業㈱ 神奈川工場 神奈川県綾瀬市 吉岡348
乳　脂　肪　分	3.2％以上
無脂乳固形分	8.0％以上
内　容　量	180ml

要冷蔵（10℃以下）　**公正**

Information panels for dairy products.

some brands of the former are thin enough to be poured.
Yogurt for eating comes in plastic containers in a wide
range of sizes. Snow, Bulgaria, Dannone, and Meito
brands are common. Containers of unflavored yogurt have
the word プレーン *purēn,* "plain," on the label. Those of
flavored yogurt have pictures of the particular fruit.

Yogurt for drinking usually comes in containers that look
like small bottles. One brand of strawberry-flavored drinking yogurt contains milk derivatives, strawberry pulp,
fruit juice, grape sugar, fruit sugar, pectin, and fruit "materials."

7 · FISH AND SEAFOOD

Fish (魚 *sakana*) and other seafood are sold in great variety at the fish market or supermarket. They come whole, filleted, or sliced; fresh, smoked, grilled, or dried; in the shell or out of the shell; swimming around in buckets, crawling around in sawdust, or packed in vacuum-sealed bags. Prices vary according to season and availability, but most fish can be bought during a large part of the year, even when not "in season" (Table 4, p. 61).

Although much fish is sold "fresh," that is, never having been frozen, an increasing proportion of the fish available has been frozen at one time. Wide-ranging fishing fleets must freeze their catches or the fish would spoil before the boats get back to port.

Because of the short life-span of uncooked fish, it is safest to use a neighborhood fish market or a large supermarket whose customers are primarily Japanese. At small grocery stores, convenience stores, and Western supermarkets, fish is not sold as quickly and may not always be very fresh. At large central fish markets where refrigeration is not common, it is a good idea to buy fish early in the day before the ice has melted and the heat of the day has taken its toll.*

Salmon, fish roe, and some shrimp may be heavily salted before sale. When salted, they may be displayed without

* Most large cities in Japan have a large central fish market, from which local retailers buy their stock. Individuals may buy directly from these markets at retail prices somewhat lower than those of local fish shops. It is an interesting experience simply to visit a central fish market—be sure to go early in the morning. (The Tokyo market is in Tsukiji, near the station of the same name on the Hibiya subway line.)

SASHIMI

refrigeration; look for the character 塩 *shio,* "salt," on the label or display sign.

In the supermarket, fish for cooking is kept in refrigerated cases near fish for eating raw *(sashimi),* but the two are not usually displayed together in the case. All whole fish, as well as other cuts of fish near the whole fish, are for cooking. Fish for eating raw is cleaned, often skinned, and displayed in bite-size slices or in larger boneless pieces to be sliced at home.

Sashimi (刺身/さしみ) refers to slices of raw fish which, when eaten, are dipped in soy sauce and often accompanied by grated *wasabi* (green horseradish) and sometimes by shredded *daikon* (white radish). *Sashimi* is often served as one of the early courses in a traditional Japanese meal. (*Sashimi* is sometimes confused with *sushi,* which refers to sweet vinegared rice accompanied by other ingredients—raw fish, raw or cooked vegetables, pickles, etc.)

Only saltwater fish and shellfish are eaten raw. Freshwater fish often carry harmful bacteria, which must be killed by cooking. Seafood commonly served as *sashimi* includes squid, tuna, scallops, prawns, sea bream, and young yellowtail. Red tuna may be the easiest form of *sashimi* to eat if one has not tried raw fish before.

Appendix 4 (p. 153) and the book *The Japanese Guide to*

Fish Cooking, listed in the Recommended Reading section, give suggestions on selecting and preparing fish.

FACTS ABOUT SOME FISH AND SEAFOOD

Bonito 鰹/かつお *katsuo*

Bonito appears in two main forms in the supermarket. From May to July it is sold fresh, both as *sashimi* and for cooking. The flesh is deep red in color. When the market prepares bonito for *sashimi,* it skins and cleans the fish and may sear the surface. The skin edge of bonito *sashimi* should always be seared before the fish is served; to do this at home, put the fish on a skewer and pass it over a gas flame. Bonito *sashimi* is usually eaten with grated ginger and chopped *naganegi* (long onion), rather than *wasabi* and *daikon.*

The more common form of this fish, however, is *katsuobushi* かつおぶし, shavings of steamed and dried bonito that could be mistaken for wood shavings. Barrels and bins of *katsuobushi* can be found at fish markets. Supermarkets sell the shavings in clear plastic, usually near the other traditional Japanese dried foods (e.g., seaweed and mushrooms). *Katsuobushi* is an ingredient in *dashi,* a soup-stock base for many Japanese dishes. It is also sprinkled plain over tofu, or mixed with powdered seaweed or sesame seeds and sprinkled over rice. These mixtures, called *furikake* ふりかけ, are sold in clear glass jars and plastic packages near the traditional foods.

Octopus たこ *tako*

Octopus is often boiled before sale. In this form its skin is maroon and its flesh dense and white. Boiled octopus is eaten like *sashimi* (octopus is never eaten raw) and is ordinarily displayed with the *sashimi* in food markets. Its presence in the refrigerator case is a good indication that

TABLE 4:

Fish Available in Japan, Their Seasons and Fat Content

Type of Fish	Season	Fat Content
Barracuda かます *kamasu*	Oct.	Part oily, part lean
Bonito 鰹/かつお *katsuo*	May–July	Oily
Carp 鯉/こい *koi*	Dec.–Feb.	Lean
Cod 鱈/たら *tara*	Jan., Feb.	Lean
Flatfish (halibut, flounder, plaice, sole)		
平目/ひらめ *hirame*	Dec.–Feb.	Lean
鰈/かれい *karei*	Apr.–July	Lean
Herring 鯡/鰊/にしん *nishin*	Winter	Oily
Horse mackerel 鯵/あじ *aji*	May–July	Oily
Lobster 伊勢海老 *ise-ebi*	Sept.–Apr.	Lean
Mackerel 鯖/さば *saba*	Sept.–Nov.	Oily
Octopus たこ *tako*	Jan.–Mar., June–Aug.	Lean
Oyster かき *kaki*	Nov.–Feb.	Lean
Perch (sillago) 鱚/きす *kisu*	Feb.–May	Lean
Pike さんま *samma*	Sept.–Nov.	Oily
Prawn 車海老 *kuruma-ebi*	Sept.–Apr.	Lean
River trout 鮎/あゆ *ayu*	June, July	Oily
Salmon 鮭/さけ or しゃけ *sake* or *shake*	May, June, Nov.	Oily
Sardine 鰯/いわし *iwashi*	Sept., Oct.	Oily
Sea bass 鱸/すずき *suzuki*	June–Aug.	Lean
Sea bream 鯛/たい *tai*	May, June, Dec.	Lean
Shrimp 海老/えび *ebi*	Sept.–Apr.	Lean
Squid (cuttlefish) いか *ika*	Oct.–June	Lean
Swordfish めかじき *mekajiki*	Winter	Lean
Trout 鱒/ます *masu*	Feb.–Apr., June–Aug.	Lean
Tuna 鮪/まぐろ *maguro*	Dec.–Feb.	Light, oily; red, lean
Yellowtail (mature stage) 鰤/ぶり *buri*	Dec.–Feb.	Oily
Yellowtail (young stage) はまち *hamachi*	Spring	Oily

OCTOPUS *(boiled)*

the fish nearby is to be eaten raw. A whole octopus is displayed with its tentacles curled under its body rather than outstretched as in monster movies. When sold sliced, the maroon skin is visible on the edge of each slice. Octopus is mild in taste and slightly rubbery in texture.

At festivals, *takoyaki* たこ焼, octopus cooked in a ball made of flour and served with a teriyaki-type sauce sprinkled with seaweed, is sold at stands under banners decorated with pictures of the animal. Even if you have no intention of eating *takoyaki,* watching it being made is worth the time.

Oysters かき *kaki*

Oysters are farmed for eating raw and often appear in the fish section of a market near the sashimi. They are sealed in a package by the wholesaler rather than the market itself, so the package will look different from packages wrapping other kinds of fish. Somewhere on the label will be the characters 生食用 *seishoku-yō,* "for eating raw." These oysters can be cooked as well.

Oysters sold in large bins at the fish market or in the same packaging as that of other fish in the supermarket are for cooking. Most oysters are sold already shelled.

Salmon 鮭/さけ or しゃけ *sake* or *shake*

Salmon comes in several varieties: fresh (生じゃけ *nama-jake*), lightly salted (甘塩 *ama-jio*); and heavily salted

(塩じゃけ *shio-jake*). Salmon is sold smoked under the name
sumōku sāmon スモーク サーモン.

Shrimp 海老/えび *ebi*

Lobsters and prawn, as well as shrimp, are referred to
by the term *ebi*. Lobsters are also called *ise-ebi* 伊勢海老
and prawns *kuruma-ebi* 車海老. The size of clawless varieties
ranges from tiny creatures no longer than a thumbnail to
giants the size of Maine lobsters. One variety is pink when
it is not cooked. *Ebi* sold out of the shell has probably
been salted (except for those to be eaten raw).

Squid いか *ika*

Various kinds of squid and cuttlefish are called *ika*.
Whole fresh squid for cooking has gray skin and can be
about 25 centimeters (10 in.) long. Before cooking a squid,
the skin, stomach, and tentacles must be removed. This is
done by holding the tip of the head in one hand and pulling
the tentacles with the other. The fishmonger will do this for
you at the fish market.

Cleaned and skinned squid is pure white. It can be cooked
or eaten raw; it therefore often appears in the market both
with the fish for cooking and with the *sashimi*. Raw squid
has a mild flavor and a consistency similar to that of a
semi-ripe avocado. Overcooked squid tends to be rubbery.

Breaded squid rings for frying are sold in the freezer case.
To my knowledge, breaded onion rings are not sold in
Japan, so breaded rings are probably squid.

Dried squid, a nutritious snack with a flavor similar to
that of smoked salmon, is sold in plastic bags displayed with
the other snacks. It is light tan in color and comes shredded.
Ikayaki いか焼, charcoal-broiled squid, is sold at festivals
and topped with a teriyaki-type sauce.

Tuna 鮪/まぐろ *maguro*

The flesh of fresh tuna comes in three colors: red, pink, and light tan; these reflect an increasing fat content. While the word *maguro* refers to tuna in general, at the fish market the term is used specifically for the low-fat red flesh, which comes from the back of the fish. Red tuna can be eaten raw, fried, or broiled. The pink flesh, medium in fattiness, is called *chūtoro* 中とろ. The light tan flesh is *toro* とろ; *toro* is good raw and in fish stews.

Phrases for the fish market

What fish is in season now?
Donna sakana ga shun desu ka?

Do you have (name of fish)?
(Name of fish) *wa arimasu ka?*

What kind of fish is this?
Kono sakana wa nan desu ka?

Is it salted?
Shio ga shite-arimasu ka?

Can it be eaten raw?
Nama de taberaremasu ka?

How many grams does it weigh?
Nan guramu arimasu ka?

About (number) of grams please.
(Number) *guramu gurai kudasai.*

How much does each one cost?*
Hitotsu ikura desu ka?

How much does it (do they) cost altogether?
Zembu de ikura desu ka?

* See Appendix 1 (pp. 143,144) for numbers used when asking for fish.

Please take off the skin. (for squid)
Kawa o muite kudasai.

Please gut the fish and remove the head. (backbone remains)
Atama to harawata o totte kudasai.

Please fillet.
Kirimi ni shite kudasai.

Counters used: HITO-KIRE   ICHI-MAI

Fish store.

8 · FLOUR

Flour available in Japan can be divided into four categories: specialty flours for baking traditional Japanese sweets; thickeners; wheat flours for breads, cakes, and tempura (i.e., batter-fried fish, vegetables, etc.); and whole-grain flours. Each of these is discussed below. All-purpose flour (a mixture of hard-wheat and soft-wheat flours) and self-rising flour are not sold in Japan. (See App. 4, p. 154, for descriptions of how to make these mixtures with available materials.)

Two common words on the front labels of bags of flour are 無添加 *mutenka,* "no additives," and 無漂白 *muhyōhaku,* "unbleached." Due to the high humidity during much of the year in many parts of Japan, it is best not to buy and store large quantities of flour in advance. Store flour in an airtight container.

Specialty Flours

Specialty flours consist of rice flours for making traditional sweets and dumplings, and bean flours for making traditional sweets. These flours are usually packaged in quantities smaller than the 1-kilogram bags used to package bread or cake flours. If you are interested in using these flours, you should consult a Japanese friend or neighbor.

Thickeners

Two products are commonly used as thickeners: cornstarch, or corn flour (コーン スターチ *kōn sutāchi*); and potato starch, or potato flour (片栗粉 *katakuri-ko*). Cornstarch comes in 400-gram (14-oz.) plastic bags that often have a picture of an ear of corn on them. Potato starch usually comes in long cylindrical paper bags of about 200 or 250 grams (7 or 9 oz.). It is stronger than cornstarch and so should be used more sparingly. The literal translation of *katakuri-ko* is "dog-tooth violet flour," but starch from the dog-tooth violet is no longer produced in sufficient quantity for general sale.

Wheat Flours 小麦粉 *komugi-ko*

Two major kinds of wheat flours are sold in Japan: hard-wheat flour, used for breads, pizza, and dinner rolls; and soft-wheat flour, used for cakes, cookies, and tempura. A separate tempura flour is also sold.

On the front label of a package of flour the brand name is written in large characters. Below this is smaller writing that tells what the flour is used for; several baked products are usually included here. The information panel often lists the kind of flour under the heading 種類 *shurui*, "kind"; and several uses under 主な用途 *omo na yōto*, "main uses."

Listed below are the main kinds of flour and some flour uses. Not all the uses for one category will appear on a given label, but enough items will be listed to indicate whether the flour is hard or soft.

Hard-wheat flour (bread flour) 強力粉 *kyōryoku-ko* is usually packaged in 1-kilogram (2 lb. 3 oz.) paper bags. Pictures of dinner rolls often appear on the package. Some of the "main uses" are as follows:

パン	*pan*, bread
手打うどん	*teuchi udon*, hand-made *udon* (noodles)
ピッツァ or ピザ	*pittsa* or *piza*, pizza
ロール	*rōru*, rolls

Soft-wheat flour (cake flour) 薄力粉 *hakuriki-ko* is also packaged in 1-kilogram paper bags. Some of the "main uses" are as follows:

ケーキ	*kēki,* cake
クッキー	*kukkii,* cookies
お菓子	*okashi,* traditional sweets
天ぷら	*tempura,* tempura

Tempura flour 天ぷら粉 *tempura-ko* contains cornstarch, baking powder, and sometimes other flours besides soft-wheat flour. This product is made specifically for tempura, so it probably should not be used in the place of soft-wheat flour for cakes and cookies. Tempura flour is usually packaged in plastic bags rather than paper ones, in weights from 300 to 700 grams (10½ oz. to 1½ lb.). A picture of tempura is often on the label.

Whole Grain Flours

Many markets carry whole-wheat, rye, and buckwheat flours as well as cornmeal. The labels for these are consistently written in English.

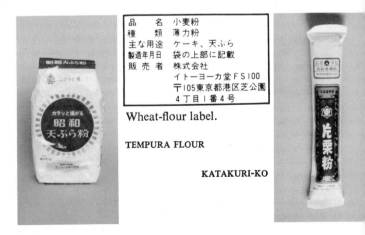

品　名　小麦粉
種　類　薄力粉
主な用途　ケーキ、天ぷら
製造年月日　袋の上部に記載
販　売　者　株式会社
　　　　　イトーヨーカ堂 FS100
　　　　　〒105東京都港区芝公園
　　　　　4丁目1番4号

Wheat-flour label.

TEMPURA FLOUR

KATAKURI-KO

⑨ · FROZEN FOOD

The Japanese prefer fresh foods, and a glance at the frozen food (冷凍食品 *reitō shokuhin*) section of any market shows the influence of demand on supply. Some frozen vegetables are sold, however, usually packaged in clear plastic or in boxes with pictures of the contents on the label. Peas, corn, string beans, mushrooms, asparagus, green soybeans in the pod, potatoes, and garlic stems are among the frozen vegetables available.

Green soybeans make a nutritious snack. Look for the word 枝豆/えだ豆 *edamame* in the information panel. (See App. 4, p. 157, for cooking instructions.) American-style potatoes come in a variety of forms and cost approximately the same per hundred grams as fresh potatoes.

Among the kinds of frozen seafood sold, squid, shrimp, clams, scallops, and eel are the most common. The packaging makes it easy to identify the product. As mentioned in Chapter 7, breaded rings are probably squid, not onions.

Prepared foods form the bulk of what is found in the frozen food department. Chinese-style dishes are the most prevalent, but Western-style hamburger patties, stuffed cabbage, and gratin dishes are also found.

Suggestions for preparing frozen foods appear in Appendix 4 (p. 154).

EDAMAME
(green soybeans)

Fresh beans on stem.

10 · JUICE

Juice (ジュース *jūsu*) is sold fresh, canned, bottled, and in frozen concentrate form. Fresh, canned, and bottled juice drinks come in various concentrations. The percentage of fruit juice (果汁 *kajū*) is indicated clearly on the label with a percent sign; percentages are given for no other ingredient in juice drinks. The word 未満 *miman* following the percentage means "less than." Most 100-percent fruit-juice products are pure juice. However, a few such products may contain added sugar (砂糖 *satō*) and flavorings. Check the *genzairyōmei* 原材料名 line of the information panel: if only one ingredient (the juice) is listed, the product is pure juice.

Fresh juice is stocked near the milk in the refrigerator cases. It comes in containers the same size and shape as milk containers, but juice containers usually bear pictures of the particular fruit. Fresh orange juice is made from *mikan* (みかん mandarin oranges) or a mixture of *mikan* and Valencia orange (バレンシア オレンジ *barenshia orenji*) juices; these words are found in the information panel, where their order indicates which kind of juice predominates. The juice of the first fruit named composes more than 50 percent of the product. To those accustomed to orange juice from other kinds of oranges, *mikan* juice may smell strong and taste thickly sweet, juice made from both *mikan* and Valencia oranges less so.

The labels of canned and bottled juice usually contain pictures of the fruit making up the juice. The name of the kind of juice is often printed in English. Bottled orange juice (*mikan* or *mikan*–Valencia orange) is common. Apple, cranberry, grape, and grapefruit juices are also available.

Grape-juice concentrate is the most common frozen concentrate found. Orange-juice concentrate exists, but is not often stocked in food markets.

品　名　天然果汁
　　　　（濃縮果汁還元）
果実名　みかん
原材料名　果汁
内容量　1000mℓ

品名　　　天然果汁（濃縮果汁還元）
果実名　　りんご
果汁含有率　果汁100%
原材料名　果汁, L-アスコルビン酸
内容量　　500ml
製造年月日　上面シール部に記載
保存温度　10℃以下
製造者　　全国農協直販㈱総合基幹工場
　　　　　千葉県印旛郡富里町
　　　　　大字高野字太木700-1

品　　名　天然果汁
　　　　　（濃縮果汁還元）
果実名　グレープフルーツ
原材料名　果汁、香料
内容量　200ml
製造年月日　キャップ上部に記載
製造者　カゴメ株式会社
　　　　　KGMW
名古屋市中区錦3丁目14-15

オレンジジュース
濃縮果汁還元　　　加糖
果汁**100%**

グレープフルーツ

品名：果汁入り清涼飲料
果実名：グレープフルーツ
原材料名：果汁, 砂糖・果
糖ぶどう糖液糖,
酸味料, 着香料
製造年月日：上部に記載
内容量：200ml
保存温度：10℃以下

要冷蔵

Juice labels and information panels.

11 · MEAT

The most common kinds of meat (肉 *niku*) in a Japanese market are chicken, pork, and beef, but ham, lamb, and veal are available in limited cuts and supplies. Various kinds of sandwich meat also are sold in most stores.

Most meat is sold boneless. In supermarkets, it is wrapped in small packages in amounts of 250 grams (9 oz.) or less. In neighborhood and specialty shops, you can ask for any amount you want. Large oven roasts are uncommon. Sliced meat ranges from chops 1 centimeter ($\frac{1}{2}$ in.) thick to sliver-thin strips. The difficulty in finding Western cuts of meat may at first pose a cooking problem. Japanese cuts lend themselves to stir-fry cooking, however, and if you enjoy Chinese dishes, you will find them easy to prepare in Japan. (See App. 4, p. 157, for a stir-fry recipe.)

Sometimes meat labels indicate the quality of the meat. The character 上 *jō* refers to high-grade meat. Middle-grade meat is 中 *chū*, but this character is rarely seen. It can be assumed that most meat is middle grade unless marked as high grade. The price also indicates the quality of the meat.

A label or sign for a specific cut of meat usually bears either the name of the meat and the cut, or the name of the meat and the suggested method of preparation. The rest of this chapter is divided into sections based on these three categories.

Kinds of Meat

Bacon ベーコン *bēkon*. Bacon comes sliced and in chunks.

Beef 牛肉 *gyūniku*. Beef comes ground and in steaks, thin slices, chunks, pot roasts, and large roasts heavily marbled with fat. Cheaper beef is lean and often tough. Good steaks demand top prices. Most beef is from domestic animals (和牛 *wagyū*); imported beef will have a sign or label bearing the word 輸入 *yunyū*, "imported."

Chicken 鶏肉/鳥肉 *toriniku*. Chicken comes in every imaginable form. Whole chickens are not commonly displayed (or very large), but you can ask for one at the poultry shop by saying, *"Tori o ichi-wa kudasai"* (Please give me one chicken). Sometimes the word 若鶏/若鳥 *waka-dori*, "young chicken," is used on labels and signs.

Duck 鴨/かも *kamo* or あひる *ahiru*. Some Western supermarkets carry duck, as do specialty shops dealing in fowl.

Ham ハム *hamu*. Ham is usually sold in small roasts. Large ham roasts are rare, but they can sometimes be found in large supermarkets at the counters where freshly sliced sandwich meat is sold. Sliced ham is the most common sandwich meat available.

Lamb ラム *ramu*. Fresh lamb is most often imported from New Zealand. It is higher in price than chicken or pork, but cheaper than beef. Frozen lamb, usually a product of Australia, is also stocked in some markets. Lamb comes in whole or boneless legs, chops, stew meat, and thin slices. The country of origin is stamped in English on the larger cuts of lamb.

Liver レバー *rebā*. Beef liver and pork liver are sold. Look on the label for the kanji for "beef" (牛) or "pork" (豚) to determine the source. Chicken livers are also sold, near the other parts of the chicken.

Pork 豚肉 *butaniku*. Pork is available ground and in long cylindrical fillets (tenderloin), boneless loins often weighing no more than 500 grams (18 oz.), tied shoulder roasts, boneless chops, slices of varying thickness, and chunks like stew meat. If you like a chop thicker than what you see at the market, buy the boneless loin and cut it to the desired thickness.

Tongue タン *tan*. Tongue is sold whole and sliced, fresh and smoked.

Turkey 七面鳥 *shichimenchō*. Imported from the United States, frozen whole turkey is available in Western supermarkets. If you do not live in a metropolitan area, you may be able to get turkey by special order (requested well in advance) at a local supermarket.

Veal 仔牛 *ko-ushi*. Veal is not commonly seen. When it is sold, it comes ground, in steaks, and in chunks.

Cuts of Meat

Beef, Pork, and Lamb

Most of the words in the following list are preceded by 牛 *gyū*, "beef," or 豚 *buta*, "pork."

ばら	*bara*, abdomen (where bacon comes from)
切身	*kirimi*, chop
ヒレ	*hire*, fillet (tenderloin)
挽肉	*hikiniku*, ground meat
合挽	*aibiki*, ground beef and pork, mixed (good for meatloaf)

もも/モモ	*momo*, leg
レバー	*rebā*, liver
ロースト	*rōsuto*, roast (for oven roasting)
肩/かた	*kata*, shoulder
ロース	*rōsu*, sirloin (whole or sliced in varying thicknesses up to that of chops)
スペア リブ	*supea ribu*, spare ribs

Chicken

正肉	*shōniku*, boneless meat with skin
骨付	*honetsuki*, with bone
胸/むね/ムネ	*mune*, breast
ささみ すじなし	*sasami sujinashi*, boneless breast without skin or tendons
もも/モモ	*momo*, leg
手羽さき	*tebasaki*, lower wing
手羽もと	*tebamoto*, upper wing
挽肉	*hikiniku*, ground chicken
すなぎも	*suna-gimo*, gizzard
きも or レバー	*kimo* or *rebā*, liver
もつ	*motsu*, various internal organs and immature eggs

Methods of Preparation

The following words are usually followed by the character 用 *yō*, "for."

バーベキュー	*bābekyū*, barbecue
カルビ焼	*karubiyaki*, barbecue, Korean style
焼肉	*yakiniku*, barbecue or sauté
バタ焼	*batayaki*, butter sauté
あみ焼	*amiyaki*, grill
しゃぶしゃぶ	*shabu-shabu* (a cook-at-the-table dish using simmering broth)

豚肩ロース焼肉用
保存温度10℃以下

super market

加工元 **株式会社 スーパーヤマザキ**
西久留米店　東京都東久留米市下里4-1-43

Ɖamazaki

加　工　日	100g当り(円)	正味量(g)	価格 (円)
61 8 10	168	306	514 (3)

Pork-for-sauté label.

ソテー	*sotē,* sauté
ステーキ	*sutēki,* steak (to be broiled, grilled, etc.)
シチュー	*shichū,* stew
すき焼	*sukiyaki,* sukiyaki (a cook-at-the-table dish in which beef and other ingredients are cooked in melted fat, sugar, and soy sauce)

Phrases for the Meat Market

Do you have a beef (pork) oven-roast?
Rōsuto biifu-(Rōsuto pōku-)yō no niku wa arimasu ka?

How many grams does it weigh?
Nan guramu arimasu ka?

(Amount) (name of animal) (name of cut), please.*
(Name of animal) *no* (name of cut) *o kudasai.*

EXAMPLES: *Buta no hire o kudasai.*
　　　　　(Pork tenderloin, please.)

　　　　　Gyū no shichū-yō o sambyaku guramu kudasai.
　　　　　(Three hundred grams of beef stewmeat, please.)

＊ See Appendix 1 (pp. 143–45) for numbers used when asking for meat and poultry.

12 · OIL AND SHORTENING

Oil 油 *abura*

Japanese markets carry a large variety of oils, some of them pure and some of them blends. Available pure oils include olive (usually imported from Italy), rice, cottonseed, safflower, peanut, and sesame oils. The names of pure oils are written in English on product labels, with the exception of sesame oil (ごま油 *goma abura*), whose labels bear either the Japanese or English words. Most pure oils come in large cans of 750 grams (1 lb. 10 oz.) or more. Olive oil also comes in smaller glass bottles, and sesame oil in small plastic and glass containers.

Two kinds of sesame oil are sold. The brown variety, used in Asian dishes, has a smoky flavor and aroma. The light yellow variety, usually imported, is tasteless and can serve as a general-purpose oil.

Blended oils are marketed as either salad oils (サラダ油 *sarada abura*) or tempura oils (天ぷら油 *tempura abura*). Tempura oils are supposed to be better than other oils for frying because they tolerate higher temperatures before smoking. Salad oils may be used for frying, but are not as heat-tolerant as tempura oils for deep frying. Blended oils come in both cans and plastic bottles.

The front label of a container of blended oils bears in a prominent position the words サラダ or 天ぷら. The *himmei* 品名 line of the information panel says simply 食用調合油 *shokuyō chōgō abura,* "blend of food oils." The specific oil content of a blend can be found in the information panel on the *genzairyōmei* 原材料名 line. The most common constituent oils are as follows (each is followed by the kanji 油):

とうもろこし or コーン	*tōmorokoshi* or *kōn*, corn
綿実	*menjitsu*, cottonseed
パーム	*pāmu*, palm
菜種/なたね	*natane*, rapeseed
紅花 or サフラワー	*benibana* or *safurawā*, safflower
大豆	*daizu*, soybean
向日葵/ひまわり or サンフラワー	*himawari* or *sanfurawā*, sunflower
植物	*shokubutsu*, vegetable

Shortening ショートニング *shōtoningu*

A vegetable shortening similar to Crisco is packaged in a metal can and displayed near the oils. The name "Snow Brand Shortening" appears on the label. This product contains hydrogenated vegetable oils and lactic acid.

SESAME OIL   **SAFFLOWER SALAD-OIL**   **TEMPURA OIL**

13 · PRODUCE

Fruit

Many markets sell two "grades" of fruit (果物 *kudamono*). Some fruit—large, unblemished, and often out of season—is sold mostly for use as gifts. The rest—everyday varieties at everyday prices—constitutes the bulk of fruit for sale.

If the skin of a fruit is to be eaten, thorough washing is recommended to remove residual pesticides. When thorough washing is difficult, such as for grapes, it might be best not to eat the skins.

Apples りんご *ringo*. Most apples are red, but Golden Delicious apples and a variety called *indo ringo* インド りんご, which looks like a Golden Delicious apple, are available. Sour green apples for cooking and baking appear only rarely. Cooking apples (料理用のりんご *ryōri-yō no ringo*), which may be slightly tart, are sold. One kind is the deep red *kōgyoku* 紅玉.

A fruit that looks like a large yellow or medium-sized brown apple appears in fall. This is actually the *nashi* (described below), an apple-like pear.

Bananas バナナ *banana*. Bananas, usually ripe by the time they reach the shelf, are available throughout most of the year.

Cherries 桜んぼ/さくらんぼ *sakurambo*. Domestically grown cherries, yellow and light red in color and smaller than Bing cherries, arrive in the market in June. In July, Bings appear.

Citrons ゆず *yuzu*. A yellow citrus fruit the size and shape of a tangerine but with thick, rough skin is available at a high price in markets, particularly in late fall and winter, when *mikan* (see below) are in season. The skin and juice of the citron are aromatic and are used not only in salads and on fish but also occasionally in bath water. The juice, called *yuzu no mizu* ゆずの水, similar in flavor to lemon juice, is sold in small bottles. It will keep for a long time in the refrigerator after the bottle is opened. A few drops of citron juice enhance the flavor of a salad dressing.

Grapefruit グレープフルーツ *gurēpufurūtsu*. Grapefruit are available beginning in early winter and last through spring. Most grapefruit are imported.

Grapes 葡萄/ぶどう *budō*. Although gift packages of grapes are available throughout the year, reasonable prices for this fruit begin in July. In June, clusters of very small reddish purple grapes appear first, followed by large round purple grapes, large round green ones, and oval red-skinned varieties. The grape season lasts into October. The larger grapes have seeds.

Kiwifruit キーウィ or キーウィフルーツ *kiiui* or *kiiuifurūtsu*. Kiwifruit are the size and shape of lemons. They have brown, slightly fuzzy skins which must be peeled. Inside is tart green fruit that can be eaten alone or blended with other fruit in a salad. Kiwifruit are available throughout the year.

Lemons レモン *remon*. Lemons are usually imported and are available year-round. Domestic varieties have more seeds and thicker skins than imported ones.

Melons メロン *meron*. Melons come in a range of sizes, from bright yellow fruit the size of a big tomato to dark green watermelon (西瓜/すいか *suika*) the size and shape of a basketball. The small *purinsu* プリンス melons, which have a pale green skin, possess a strong odor that permeates the refrigerator.

Gift melons are sold throughout the year, but the melon season begins in June. Watermelon, when in the peak of the season in July and August, is the best buy in melons.

Mikan みかん. The word *mikan* is a general term for native varieties of oranges, but it is most commonly used to refer to the small mandarin orange (tangerine), the sweet and juicy staple fruit of winter. Early in fall, when these *mikan* first come to the stores, they are dark green and slightly tart. Within a few weeks, they turn yellow and then orange, to remain that way until they disappear in early spring.

The natural coloring of *mikan* is strong and tends to give an orange cast to the skin of children who eat a lot of them or drink a lot of orange juice. The palms of the hands and soles of the feet are particularly affected.

Other varieties of *mikan* come out as the regular *mikan* are finishing, sometimes as early as mid-February, and remain in the market until May. They are sold loose and in red nets. All are easiest to eat if the skin of each inner section is removed after the fruit is peeled. The four most common varieties, in approximate order of increasing size and sourness, are *iyokan* 伊予柑, *hassaku* はっさく, *amanatsu* 甘夏, and *natsumikan* 夏みかん.

Nashi 梨/なし. *Nashi* are sometimes called "pear-apples" because they look like apples and taste somewhat like pears. They are juicy and sweet. Two varieties are available; both appear in early fall and disappear by November, except in the gift-fruit section of the market. The yellow-skinned variety (二十世紀 *nijusseiki*) looks like a large Golden Delicious apple. The other variety has a rough brown skin.

Oranges オレンジ *orenji*. The word *orenji* refers to varieties of oranges such as navels and Valencias that were originally imported from the West. Most still are, but some are now grown domestically. These oranges are sold from winter through late spring, after the main stock of *mikan* starts to dwindle.

Peaches 桃/もも *momo*. Pale yellowish green to yellow and red in color, peaches are available at the height of summer. The tastiest varieties are the *hakutō* 白桃 and the *suimitsutō* 水蜜桃.

Persimmons 柿/かき *kaki*. In fall, a bright orange, smooth-skinned fruit appears in two shapes, one like a miniature pumpkin, the other like a plum tomato. These are persimmons, delicate and sweet to the taste. Some have tiny brown marks on the skin, which may also appear inside; these affect the appearance but not the taste. Some persimmons are seedless; others have smooth flat brown seeds. Persimmons should be peeled.

From December to early February, dried persimmons (ほし柿 *hoshi-gaki*) are sold.

Pineapples パイナップル *painappuru*. Pineapples are available throughout the year; their price hardly fluctuates. Some pineapples are grown domestically, in Okinawa, but most are imported from the Philippines, Taiwan, and Hawaii.

YUZU *(citrons)*

AMANATSU

BIWA
(loquat)

MIKAN
(mandarin oranges)

PURINSU MERON
("prince" melon)

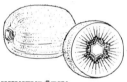

KIIUIFURŪTSU
(kiwifruit)

NASHI *(pear-apple)*

KAKI *(persimmons)*

UME *(green plums)*

Plums プラム *puramu*. Plums make their appearance toward the end of June and last through summer. The most common are yellow and red in color. The term *sumomo* すもも is used for certain plums.

The round green "plums" (梅 *ume*) that grow on Japanese "plum" trees are really members of the apricot family. They come to the market in June, packaged in large plastic bags. The Japanese make pickles and wine from them. The fruit is sour and is not to be eaten fresh.

Strawberries 苺/いちご *ichigo*. The best season for strawberries is late January until March, but they are also sold at fairly reasonable prices later in spring and in early summer. They are a welcome harbinger of spring as they sit primly in their plastic containers.

Other Fruit

Other varieties of fresh fruit available during the year include figs (いちじく *ichijiku*), litchis (れいし *reishi*), loquats (びわ *biwa*), pomegranates (ざくろ *zakuro*), pears (西洋なし *seiyō nashi*), blueberries (ブルーベリー *burūberii*) cranberries (クランベリー *kuranberii*), mangoes (マンゴー *mangō*), papayas (パパイヤ *papaiya*), and raspberries (ラズベリー *razuberii*). Some rare fruits that look like genetic experimentations appear occasionally. Throughout the year many markets sell dried fruit, usually imported, including apricots, dates, prunes, and raisins.

Vegetables

Unlike the fruit sold in Japan, most vegetables (野菜 *yasai*) are sold in one grade or quality. Ginger, potatoes, spinach, and tomatoes are a few exceptions. Vegetables cost more when they are out of season, but the temperate climate of most of the country results in short out-of-season periods.

Asparagus アスパラガス *asuparagasu*. Asparagus is available fresh for a brief period in spring and again in fall. It also comes frozen and canned.

Bamboo Shoots 竹の子/たけのこ *takenoko*. When bamboo shoots spring up from the ground, they wear a brown, hairy outer series of layers which must be removed before the shoot is cooked. Fresh bamboo shoots arrive in the market in March and last until about May. Their bitterness is best removed by boiling them in the water drained off when rice is washed. Fresh bamboo shoots should never be eaten raw, because they contain cyanide, which the cooking process removes.

During much of the year, markets sell the shoots already boiled. In this form they are a creamy white color. Sometimes they are cut in half at the market, so that a curious ladder-like series of membranes can be seen down the middle of the plant. Before being used, pre-boiled bamboo shoots should be cut in half (if the market has not already done so) and then must be washed thoroughly.

Canned bamboo shoots (pre-boiled) are also available, but taste rather different from the fresh ones.

Bean Sprouts もやし *moyashi*. Two kinds of bean sprouts are widely available. The smaller kind come from the mung bean, the larger from the soybean. Sold year-round, the sprouts are packaged in clear plastic and kept in the refrigerated section of larger markets. They are highly perishable and should be used within two days of purchase. One of the cheapest vegetables at the market, bean sprouts can be used either fresh in salads or quickly cooked as a dinner vegetable.

A third and rarer bean sprout grown from alfalfa seeds is occasionally seen. This sprout is far more delicate than the other two and should not be cooked. It can be used in salads and sandwiches.

Broccoli ブロッコリー *burokkorii*. Broccoli seems to come in and out of the market at random. The price varies throughout the year.

Brussels Sprouts 芽キャベツ *mekyabetsu*. Brussels sprouts are in season in mid-winter, although they may be available occasionally at other times of the year.

Cabbage キャベツ *kyabetsu*. Regular cabbage is grown and sold year-round. Chinese cabbage (白菜 *hakusai*), a vegetable with longer leaves and a milder taste than regular cabbage, is also available throughout the year. Both kinds of cabbage are staple winter vegetables.

Carrots 人参/にんじん *ninjin*. Except for a brief period in spring, carrots are in good supply year-round. They are sometimes as large as 8 centimeters (3 in.) in diameter. Two varieties can be found in the market. One, the same color orange as a *mikan,* has a stubby tip; the other, the color of a winter tomato, has a pointed tip.

Cauliflower カリフラワー *karifurawā*. Cauliflower is in

season during mid-winter but can be bought at other times of the year as well. When in season, cauliflower is reasonable in price.

Celery セロリー *serorii.* Celery is sold by the bunch, by the single stalk, and between these two extremes. It is often high in price. Celery is not as popular a vegetable as some and may be difficult to find at times.

Corn とうもろこし *tōmorokoshi.* Fresh corn on the cob is sold during the summer. Frozen and canned corn are widely available.

Cucumbers きゅうり *kyūri.* Japanese cucumbers are usually about 20 centimeters (8 in.) long and only 2½ centimeters (1 in.) in diameter. They are available throughout the year. Because the skin is not waxed, cucumbers need not be peeled, but they should be washed thoroughly.

Daikon 大根. In Japan, some vegetables are either much larger or much smaller than similar varieties in the West. The *daikon,* a kind of radish, is an example of the former par excellence. This white root is sometimes 60 centimeters (2 ft.) long and 5 centimeters (2 in.) in diameter. It has the same shape and taste as an icicle radish. *Daikon* are available at all times of the year, but may be bitter between February and April. The Japanese use *daikon* in salads, stews, and, grated, as a flavoring with tempura and other dishes. *Daikon* are also used to make various pickles such as the yellow *takuan.* It is thought that raw *daikon* helps to digest fatty foods.

Small red radishes (called *radishu* ラディシュ) can be found occasionally at some markets.

Eggplant なす *nasu*. Japanese eggplant comes in two sizes: small but relatively long, and short and stubby. Eggplants are most commonly pickled, or fried as part of a tempura meal. The large Western variety of eggplant, for such dishes as eggplant Parmesan, may be difficult to find, but are becoming more common.

Garlic にんにく *ninniku*. Individual cloves on a head of garlic are large but mild. One of these cloves can be safely used in a Western recipe calling for a clove of garlic.

Garlic stems にんにくの茎 *ninniku no kuki*. Garlic stems are about $\frac{1}{2}$ centimeter ($\frac{1}{4}$ in.) in diameter and come in various lengths starting from 15 centimeters (6 in.). They are available both fresh and frozen. Unlike garlic cloves, the stems are not highly aromatic and are sweet when cooked.

Ginger しょうが *shōga*. Japanese cuisine uses ginger in a variety of ways, and the plant is available in a variety of forms in the market. Ginger root can be found in the fresh produce section throughout the year. The root is a gnarled object about $2\frac{1}{2}$ centimeters (1 in.) in diameter with several short, blunt ends. When young, its skin is light tan, translucent, and almost shiny. The skin becomes dark tan, opaque, dry, and slightly wrinkled as the root ages.

Young ginger shoots are in season in late April and early May, but are found occasionally at other times of the year. These shoots have long green stems that grow from a pink and cream-colored root about 1 centimeter ($\frac{1}{2}$ in.) in diameter. Ginger shoots are considerably mild in taste compared to the root.

Pickled ginger, dyed pink or red with red perilla leaves

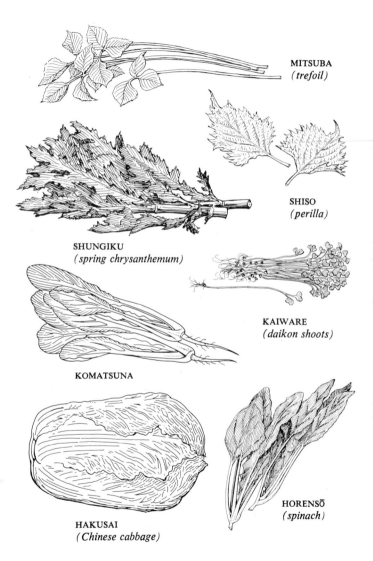

MITSUBA
(trefoil)

SHISO
(perilla)

SHUNGIKU
(spring chrysanthemum)

KAIWARE
(daikon shoots)

KOMATSUNA

HAKUSAI
(Chinese cabbage)

HORENSŌ
(spinach)

or artificial color, is sold in clear plastic bags. Pickled ginger may be cut in short julienne-like strips (served, for example, with curried rice) or in thin flat shavings (served with *sushi*).

Grated ginger can be made at home from fresh ginger root, but it is also available in jars and tubes near the spices. Grated ginger accompanies certain kinds of *sashimi* (e.g., bonito) and is put in tempura sauce along with grated *daikon*.

All forms of ginger—fresh, pickled, and pre-grated—should be refrigerated at home. Powdered ginger is never used as a substitute when a recipe for a Japanese dish calls for ginger.

Ginkgo nuts ぎんなん *ginnan*. When sold in the shell, ginkgo nuts are about 2 centimeters ($\frac{3}{4}$ in.) in diameter, slightly elliptic in shape, and white in color. When sold without their shells, the nuts look like brown acorns; the brown color comes from a thin skin which must be removed. The flesh of ginkgo nuts is light green before being cooked; it becomes slightly darker with cooking. Ginkgo nuts are a common ingredient in the dinner custard called *chawan-mushi*.

Ginkgo nuts, already shelled, skinned, and boiled, are sold in cans. They are different in flavor and consistency from the fresh nuts.

Kaiware かいわれ. These greens, available in winter, are the young shoots of the *daikon*. They look like two-petaled clovers on a stem about 10 centimeters (4 in.) long. The shoots have a slightly peppery taste and often serve as a garnish for *sashimi*. They can be used in salads.

Lettuce レタス *retasu*. Lettuce comes in many varieties, including iceberg, endive, and Boston. It is especially plentiful in early summer, but can be bought throughout the year.

Lotus Root 蓮根 *renkon*. Fresh lotus root is usually sold in lengths of about 8 to 15 centimeters (3 to 6 in.) and is about 5 centimeters (2 in.) in diameter. Its exterior is slightly tan and should be peeled or scraped before the vegetable is used. A wagon-wheel design running down the center of the root gives beauty to the vegetable when it is sliced. Lotus root is almost tasteless, but always crunchy. It is commonly used in tempura and stir-fried in Chinese-style dishes. It is available during much of the year.

Mushrooms 茸/きのこ *kinoko* or 茸/たけ *take*. Most mushrooms in Japan are brown, and most of the varieties discussed below are sold year-round. The most common mushroom is called *shiitake* (椎茸/しいたけ). The fresh form (生しいたけ *nama-shiitake*) has a flat brown velvety cap about 5 centimeters (2 in.) in diameter. The stem is tough and is best cut off and discarded. The dried form (ほし椎茸 *hoshi-shiitake*) has more flavor than the fresh mushroom. It can be soaked in water for a few hours and used as fresh. *Shiitake* can be used in soups, stews, and stir-fried dishes.

White button mushrooms are called *masshurūmu* マッシュルーム. Fresh ones can be found at some markets, but canned and frozen ones are more widely available. In recipes calling for white mushrooms, Japanese mushrooms may not always be good substitutes.

A mushroom called *matsutake* 松茸 is sold in autumn. *Matsutake* are much larger than *shiitake* and claim an enormous price, although some storekeepers sell small portions at lower prices. The *matsutake* is highly valued for its rich flavor.

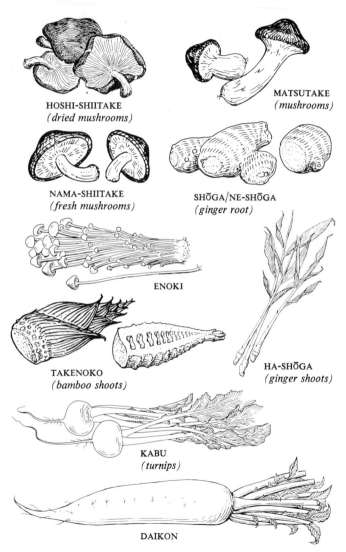

HOSHI-SHIITAKE
(dried mushrooms)

MATSUTAKE
(mushrooms)

NAMA-SHIITAKE
(fresh mushrooms)

SHŌGA/NE-SHŌGA
(ginger root)

ENOKI

TAKENOKO
(bamboo shoots)

HA-SHŌGA
(ginger shoots)

KABU
(turnips)

DAIKON

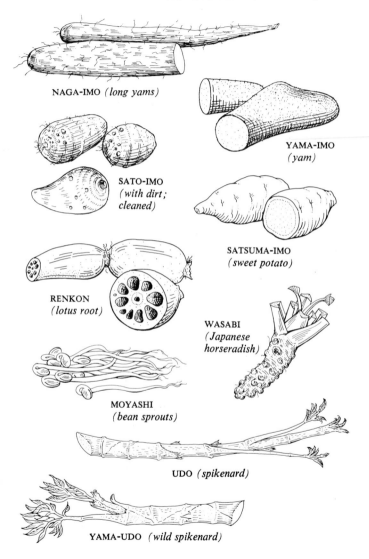

NAGA-IMO *(long yams)*

YAMA-IMO
(yam)

SATO-IMO
*(with dirt;
cleaned)*

SATSUMA-IMO
(sweet potato)

RENKON
(lotus root)

WASABI
*(Japanese
horseradish)*

MOYASHI
(bean sprouts)

UDO *(spikenard)*

YAMA-UDO *(wild spikenard)*

Enoki えのき are small, slender white mushrooms sold in bunches and usually wrapped in plastic bags. They are used in sukiyaki, stews, and other dishes. Although they are not very flavorful, they enhance the appearance of a dish.

Naganegi 長ねぎ. *Naganegi* are long green onions similar in appearance to leeks. They are up to about 40 centimeters (16 in.) long and $2\frac{1}{2}$ centimeters (1 in.) in diameter. They are used in sukiyaki, in stir-fried dishes, and in other dishes in the place of onions; the white part of the *naganegi* is eaten and the green leaves discarded. Large bunches of *naganegi* covered with soil are sold in winter at cheaper prices in some markets.

A related vegetable is *nira* にら, relatively short, thin, flat green leaves used in stir-fried dishes. Leeks (リーク *riiku*) are also available at times.

Onions 玉ねぎ *tamanegi*. The common onion with light brown skin is widely available. Red onions (赤ねぎ *akanegi*) can also be found at some markets. Pearl onions are found occasionally.

Peas えんどう豆 *endōmame*. Peas are available fresh in early summer. They are often sold already shelled. Frozen peas are one of the more widely distributed frozen vegetables.

Snow peas (さやえんどう *saya-endō*) are found in markets during a large part of the year. The pods as well as the peas inside are eaten. Snow peas can be lightly stir-fried or used uncooked in fresh salad. Soaking them in water will make them crisp.

Peppers ピーマン *piiman*. Although small versions of the bell pepper can be found in markets, the more common green pepper has a thinner wall and a pointed tip. Peppers are packaged in plastic bags and are available throughout much of the year.

A small pepper about 5 centimeters (2 in.) long that looks like a green chili pepper is also sold. Called *shishitō* ししとう, this pepper is usually sweet, although sometimes a single hot one is found in a package. *Shishitō* are used in tempura and are grilled as a side dish accompanying grilled fish.

Perilla しそ *shiso*. The perilla, or beefsteak plant, is a serrate leaf about 8 centimeters (3 in.) wide at the base. Green perilla leaves, available year-round, are sold in bunches of about five. They possess a distinctive flavor and are often served with *sashimi,* in tempura, and in salads. The purple-red variety, used to color pickled plums and ginger, is seen in the market in May and June.

Potatoes 芋/いも *imo*. The word *imo* is a general term for potatoes, yams, and taros. The white potatoes commonly found in the West are called *jaga-imo* じゃがいも. All potatoes in Japan can be baked or fried but most varieties disintegrate easily when boiled. To determine whether a potato is good for boiling, dissolve 2 tablespoons salt in $1\frac{3}{8}$ American cups (330 ml.) water in a small bowl. Put the whole potato in the solution. If it floats, it can be boiled successfully.

Several other tubers and roots called *imo* are best avoided by those who do not like slimy vegetables. The taro (里いも *sato-imo* or タロ *taro*) is about 5 centimeters (2 in.) in diameter, round, and usually covered with dirt or dark skin. Taros also come white, peeled, and packaged in liquid in plastic bags in the refrigerated section of the produce department. They then look like small peeled potatoes.

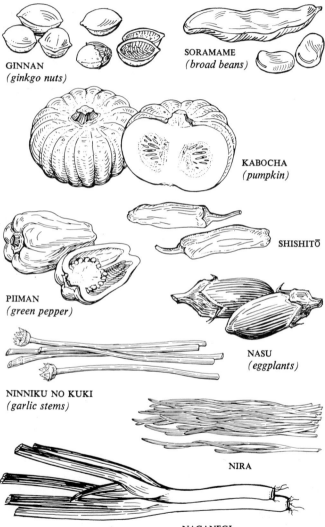

GINNAN
(ginkgo nuts)

SORAMAME
(broad beans)

KABOCHA
(pumpkin)

SHISHITŌ

PIIMAN
(green pepper)

NASU
(eggplants)

NINNIKU NO KUKI
(garlic stems)

NIRA

NAGANEGI

Two other varieties of *imo* are the *yama-imo* 山いも (or *yama-no-imo*) and the *naga-imo* 長いも, both species of yam. They have tan skin that looks like the skin of a new potato but with hairs growing out of the surface. The *yama-imo* has an irregular shape; the *naga-imo* is quite long, sometimes up to 1 meter (1 yd.). These yams secrete a thick liquid in the same way that okra does. Both are grated to make *tororo,* which is like Hawaiian poi.

Pumpkin and **Squash** かぼちゃ *kabocha.* Pumpkins in Japan have dark green skins and yellow flesh. Usually no larger than 10 centimeters (4 in.) high and 15 centimeters (6 in.) in diameter, they are sold whole or cut in half or quartered. They are most abundant in winter, but last through late spring. Most varieties are like butternut squash in texture and flavor, although one variety has the texture and appearance of acorn squash. Pumpkin can be used in tempura, baked in the oven (plain or stuffed with meat), or steamed with the skin on.

Zucchini is sometimes sold in the market, but not in large quantities. Winter squash, butternut, and yellow summer squash are not available.

Rape blossoms 菜の花 *nanohana.* The tips of rape blossoms resemble those of broccoli, but the stems of the former are thinner. Rape blossoms are sold in bunches. They have a slightly bitter taste if overcooked.

Spikenard うど *udo.* This vegetable is a pale green and maroon stalk that looks like sugar cane and resembles celery in texture and taste. It is used uncooked in salads, but should be soaked slightly in vinegared water before so using. A more cheaply priced variety is called *yama-udo* 山うど.

Spinach ほうれん草 *hōrensō*. Two kinds of spinach are available during much of the year. Both have flat, flexible leaves that come to a few points, and both taste about the same. Fresh spinach can be used raw in salads, cooked in soup, or stir-fried with other vegetables. Spinach needs to be cooked for only a brief time.

A leafy vegetable that comes in bunches and looks somewhat like spinach is called *komatsuna* 小松菜. This vegetable is boiled in soup stock, but is not eaten raw.

Spring chrysanthemums 春菊 *shungiku*. This is a green vegetable whose leaves look somewhat like those of the true chrysanthemum. Available throughout the year, the spring chrysanthemum is sold in bunches near the other greens in a market. It is cooked briefly in such dishes as sukiyaki and in clear soups and *miso* soup.

String beans さやいんげん *saya-ingen*. String beans do not seem to have a special season. They are sold fresh, but are more frequently available in the frozen-food department of a market.

A plant that looks like a large fat string bean begins its season in mid-May. This is the broad bean, or horse bean (そら豆 *soramame*). The beans should be removed from the pod and cooked in salted water.

Sweet potatoes さつまいも *satsuma-imo*. Sweet potatoes in Japan have reddish purple skins. The ones that appear in spring are small and thin, about 15 centimeters (6 in.) long. The fall varieties are about as long as Japanese eggplant and as wide as a white potato. All sweet potatoes have pale yellow flesh and a mild flavor. Sweet potatoes are best prepared by being washed, cut into pieces, and steamed with the skins on. When they are baked in the oven, they should be wrapped in foil; otherwise, the skin becomes hard and crisp long before the inside is cooked. Sliced sweet potatoes are often used in tempura.

Sweet potatoes taste best when bought from the *yaki-imo* man. In fall and winter you will hear his plaintive cry during the late afternoon and early evening as he drives his truck or pulls his cart through town selling his wares. Buy one *yaki-imo* for each person and reheat the potatoes at home in the oven, if necessary. Carrying the *yaki-imo* home helps to keep the hands warm.

In addition to the above, American-style sweet potatoes can be bought canned.

Tomatoes トマト *tomato*. During much of the year, the tomatoes in the market are red with soft flesh. Dark red tomatoes that look vine ripened are available during the summer months. Cherry tomatoes (チェリー トマト *cherii tomato*) are tart and claim high prices in winter.

Trefoil 三ッ葉 *mitsuba*. This plant has a long stem topped by three leaves with serrated edges. Several kinds are sold, varying in size, shade of green, and apparent delicateness. Trefoil is added to dinner custard *(chawan-mushi)* at the end of the cooking process. It can be served in salads and clear soups. Cilantro, or fresh coriander (コサイ *kosai*), is sold in some markets, usually near the trefoil. Cilantro's strong odor distinguishes it from the odorless trefoil, but the leaves of the two plants are almost identical.

Turnips かぶ *kabu*. Turnips in Japan are pure white and usually about 5 centimeters (2 in.) in diameter. They are high in water content and should be steamed rather than boiled in water. They cook quickly. Raw turnip can be used in salads. Turnip, cooked or raw, tastes like *daikon*.

Wasabi わさび. A kind of horseradish, *wasabi* is green with a somewhat brown exterior. The plant is about 10 centimeters (4 in.) long and 2½ centimeters (1 in.) wide at the top, tapering to a blunt tip. At the market it is usually kept in water. *Wasabi* is available throughout the year.

Powdered *wasabi* is sold in small cans and in plastic bags found near the spices or mustards. The powder must be mixed with a small amount of water. *Wasabi* is also sold in tubes, which must be refrigerated after being opened.

The most common use of *wasabi* (peeled and grated fresh, or reconstituted or from the tube) is as a flavoring for the soy sauce accompanying *sashimi*. *Wasabi* can be used as a substitute for white horseradish, although the two differ somewhat in flavor.

Other Vegetables

Fresh okra, beets, artichokes, and avocados are sometimes seen. Beets and artichoke hearts can be bought canned. Burdock (ごぼう *gobō*), a long root sold sometimes with the dirt still on it, is a common sight at the produce market. It does not lend itself well to Western cooking. Fresh chestnuts (栗 *kuri*) can be bought in the fall; roasted chestnuts (甘栗 *ama-guri*) are available from pushcarts in winter and at festivals during other times of the year. Although too numerous to describe here individually, varieties of green leafy vegetables native to the Far East are sold throughout the year.

GOBŌ *(burdock)*

14 · RICE

Rice (米 *kome*) is usually packaged in plastic bags in amounts of up to 10 kilograms (22 lb.). The price of rice is fixed by the government, so the unit price of a given variety of rice is uniform, or nearly so, regardless of the quantity being bought. All rice in Japan is short-grain rice, which has an aroma and texture different from the long-grain rice grown in most of the world. Three kinds of rice are available: white, brown, and *haiga* rice.

White rice 白米 *hakumai* is the most common. Cooked white short-grain rice is stickier and easier to eat with chopsticks than the long-grain kind. Several grades and varieties are available. Two of the more expensive high-grade varieties are *koshihikari* コシヒカリ from Niigata Prefecture and *sasanishiki* ササニシキ from Yamagata Prefecture. Such names are prominently displayed in Japanese writing on the bag.

Brown rice 玄米 *gemmai* is rice from which the germ and the brown bran around the grain have not been removed. Brown rice has a nutty flavor and coarser texture than white rice. It is considered poor-man's rice in Japan, somewhat in the way that brown bread used to be considered poor-man's bread in Europe.

Haiga rice 胚芽精米 *haiga seimai* has been partially refined so that the bran has been removed but the germ *(haiga)* remains. *Haiga* rice can be cooked like white rice, but should not be washed or the germ will separate from the rice and go down the drain. The most easily identified brand of *haiga* rice bears a large "V" followed by a small "B + E."

When short-grain rice is cooked, a proportion of water smaller than that used for cooking long-grain rice is required. (See App. 4, p. 155, for washing and cooking instructions for the three kinds of rice mentioned above.)

| SASANISHIKI | KOSHIHIKARI | GEMMAI |

Rice store.

15 · SALT AND SUGAR

Salt

Salt (塩 *shio*) is sold in boxes, plastic bags, plastic cylindrical containers, and small glass jars. Salt may be bleached or unbleached, moist or dry, coarse or granular. Since most salt is sold in see-through packages, it is possible to detect the nature of the product by its appearance; bleached salt is noticeably whiter than the unbleached kind. The package usually states prominently the actual percentage of salt in the product (95 percent for coarser grades to 99.5 percent for the most refined). Salt sold in Japan is not iodized, since iodine is found in fish and seaweed, two important components of the Japanese diet.

Salt for table use, *shokutaku-en* 食卓塩, is always dry. The small glass jars of *shokutaku-en* can be refilled from plastic bags of the product or of *seisei-en* 精製塩 "refined salt."

Salt for general use, such as for cooking, is labeled as either 食塩 *shokuen,* "salt," or 家庭用塩 *katei-yō shio,* "salt for household use"; packages of the latter often bear the words "kitchen salt." The coarser and moister grades of this kind of salt are used for pickling, not cooking.

For those on low-sodium diets, salt substitute is available in small glass jars in larger markets. Look for a long list of ingredients on the jar, the first two of which are 塩化カリウム *enka karyūmu,* "potassium chloride," (about 65 percent) and 塩化ナトリウム *enka natoryūmu,* "sodium chloride" (about 35 percent).

A related product is monosodium glutamate (msg.), which

comes in small glass jars, cans, and plastic bags. Its generic name is *kagaku chōmiryō;* the most common brand is 味の素 *ajinomoto.* A mixture of salt and msg. is sold under the name アジシオ *ajishio.*

Some products are either reduced in salt or salt free. The front label of such items will bear one of the following words:

うす塩 or 甘塩	*usu-jio* or *ama-jio,* low salt
減塩	*gen'en,* very low salt
無塩	*muen,* salt free

It is not always clear just how low in salt low-salt products are. If salt is a major concern, it is safer to buy salt-free products.

Sugar

Sugar (砂糖 *satō*) is usually sold in clear plastic bags, 1 kilogram (2 1b. 3 oz.) or less in size.

Brown sugar ブラウン シュガー *buraun shugā.* Brown sugar for cooking and baking comes in two shades, light and very dark. Both are usually moist and finely ground, although lumps are sometimes found. The two kinds are different in flavor.

Brown sugar for coffee (コーヒー用 シュガー *kōhii-yō shugā*) comes in lumps and crystals of various sizes, visible through the package.

Confectioners' sugar 粉糖 *funtō.* Confectioners' sugar is available in 400-gram (14-oz.) clear plastic bags. It may need to be sifted before being used.

Cube sugar 角砂糖 *kaku-zatō*. Sugar cubes for tea and coffee are sold in boxes and plastic bags. The cubes come in several sizes.

Granulated sugar グラニュー糖 *guranyū-tō*. Labels of some brands of granulated sugar for table use bear the words "table sugar." A moister grade of granulated sugar, called *shiro-zatō* 白砂糖 (lit., white sugar), is made for cooking purposes. If it is used for baking, the liquid called for in the recipe should be reduced slightly.

Rock sugar 氷砂糖 *kōri-zatō*. Rock sugar is sold in large semi-transparent chunks or smaller flat cubes, mostly for making wine. Recipes for plum wine are found in some Japanese cookbooks.

Sugar substitutes. Several brands of sugar substitutes are available. One, with the word "fructose" on the label, is a natural product. Other brands are chemical sweeteners.

TABLE SALT   WHITE SUGAR *(moist)*   GRANULATED SUGAR

16 · TEA

There are three main kinds of tea: unfermented, or green; fermented, or black; and semi-fermented, or oolong. Japanese teas, rich in calcium, phosphorus, and vitamins A and C, are all unfermented. Most tea drunk in the West has been fermented; Chinese teas include all three types. Like fermented teas, unfermented teas contain tannic acid and caffeine.

Japanese Tea お茶 *ocha*

Japanese tea comes in leaf and powdered form, the latter used mostly for the tea ceremony. Leaf tea is sold loose, in plastic and foil bags, in cans, and in tea bags. There are several grades of leaf tea, the highest and most expensive being *gyokuro* 玉露, followed by *sencha* 煎茶. Another high-grade tea is *shincha* 新茶 "new tea," which is tea made from the first leaves of the harvest. *Shincha* is sold in the spring. One of these high-grade teas should be used if you wish to serve Japanese guests green tea.

The next grade is *bancha* 番茶, made from less tender leaves than those used for *sencha*. This is the tea served in most small Japanese restaurants and the most common kind drunk at home with meals. There are several other popular teas for home use. *Gemmaicha* 玄米茶 is green tea mixed with roasted and popped brown rice, visible in the plastic bag in which the tea is sold. *Gemmaicha* has a nutty flavor. *Hōjicha* ほうじ茶 is made from green tea leaves that have been roasted to a brown color. It is not as bitter as green tea and has a smoky aroma. Some neighborhood tea shops roast the tea on the premises; this is the best kind.

Powdered tea (抹茶 *matcha*), used for the tea ceremony, comes in small packages and in cans. This kind of tea can be bitter and is not drunk on a day-to-day basis by most people.

In the summer, *mugicha* 麦茶, a cold drink made from roasted barley (and no tea) is a common drink. It comes in loose form and in large tea bags. Most kinds can be made by simply immersing the bag in cold water. If a large amount is made, it should be refrigerated; any tea left over at the end of the day is best discarded. Sweetened powdered green tea is also available for use as a cold drink in summer.

In general, it is best to buy only as much tea as you know you will use in the near future, as tea can become moldy in times of high humidity. Tea leaves can be refrigerated in a sealed container.

Black Tea 紅茶 *kōcha*

Many brands of black tea are available in markets. Most brands have labels in English. The word ブレンド国 *burendo-koku,* "country of blending [the tea leaves]," appears in the information panel of many labels, in addition to the country of origin. Black tea is usually blended in England.

Chinese Tea

Chinese teas such as oolong (烏龍茶/ウーロン茶 *ūroncha*) and jasmine (ジャスミン茶 *jasumincha*) can be found in many markets.

Instructions for brewing Japanese tea can be found in *Japanese Cooking: A Simple Art,* listed in the Recommended Reading section.

17 · VINEGAR AND SAUCES

This chapter contains information on vinegar (酢 *su*) and a miscellaneous selection of sauces divided into the following categories: meat sauces, prepared cooking sauces, and Western sauces (ketchup, mayonnaise, applesauce, etc.). Except for the last type, sauces, along with vinegar, are likely to be displayed near one another in a market.

Vinegar

Because Japanese vinegar is lower in acidity than most Western brands, it does not need to be diluted as much as Western vinegar. It can be used successfully as is in salad dressings and in recipes calling for vinegar. To determine the degree of acidity of a particular brand or kind of vinegar, look in the information panel for the character 酸 *san,* "acid." Next to it will appear the percentage of acidity. Japanese vinegar is usually below 4.5 percent, Western brands around 5 percent.

Listed below are some of the kinds of vinegar available. These names are listed in the information panel on the *himmei* 品名 line. Sometimes the English term appears on the front label.

酢 or 穀物酢	*su* or *kokumotsu-su,* plain vinegar, made from grain
りんご酢	*ringo-su,* cider vinegar
米酢	*yone-zu/kome-zu,* rice vinegar
ぽん酢	*pon-zu,* citron vinegar (used as a dipping sauce for dishes cooked at the table)

ワイン ビネガー   *wain binegā*, wine vinegar
すし酢   *sushi-zu*, sweetened vinegar (used in making *sushi*)

Sauces

Meat Sauces

Meat sauces, sold in glass or plastic bottles of about 300 milliliters (10 fl. oz.), come in three basic thicknesses; an indication of the thickness appears on the front label of the container. *Tonkatsu* とんかつ sauce, the thickest, is made for the fried breaded pork cutlet of the same name. It also goes well with *yakisoba* (fried noodles). *Chūkoi* 中濃, "middle thickness," sauce is good with hamburgers and fried food. The thinnest sauce is Worcestershire sauce, called *usutā* ウスター.

Prepared Cooking Sauces

Many kinds of prepared cooking sauces are available at the food market. Most of these are for curries, stews, or Chinese-style dishes. The sauces come in boxes about 15 by 11 by 1 centimeters (6 by $4\frac{1}{2}$ by $\frac{1}{2}$ in.), or in cans the size of soup cans. The canned sauces and some of the boxed varieties are ready for use and need only be heated. Many of the other boxed sauces, however, are in powder or roux form. The roux is stirred into the main ingredients (meat, vegetables, etc.) and water. Pictures of ingredients are shown on the label. The amount of water can be found in the instructions on the back of the package. (See App. 3, p. 152, for terms used in cooking instructions.)

Western Sauces

Ketchup (ケチャップ *kechappu*) and mayonnaise (マヨ

ネーズ *mayonēzu*) are common items in a market and are often found near one another on the shelves. They are packaged in clear plastic squeeze bottles that often bear labels in English. Although the ketchup tastes much like that in the West, the mayonnaise tastes different from mayonnaise sold elsewhere.

Mustard (マスタード *masutādo* or 洋がらし *yō-garashi*) is usually stocked on the same shelves as ketchup and mayonnaise. Many imported and domestic brands are available. Mustard is sold powdered (in jars, cans, and plastic bags) and prepared (in jars). (Japanese mustard, *karashi* からし or *wa-garashi* 和がらし, darker and hotter than Western mustard, is also available in these forms and in small tubes.)

Cranberry sauce and applesauce can be found on the shelves near meat sauces, but only in large supermarkets. No domestic brands exist.

品　　　名	レトルトパウチ食品 （中華合わせ調味料）
原　材　料	トマトケチャップ、大豆油 醸造酢、清酒、しょうが 澱粉、砂糖、リンゴピューレ 食塩、豆板醤、にんにく 醤油、化学調味料
殺菌方法	加圧加熱殺菌
内　容　量	110g（3〜4人分）
製造年月日	欄外右下に記載
調理方法	欄外真上に記載
販　売　者	味の素株式会社NY 東京都中央区京橋1の5の8

Information panel for prepared sauce.

RICE VINEGAR　　TONKATSU SAUCE

18 · TRADITIONAL FOODS

With the exception of noodles, soy sauce, and perhaps tofu, the traditional foods described in this chapter may be new to most Western readers when they first arrive in Japan. It is possible to live and cook in Japan for any number of years and never buy one of these foods in the market. It will be more difficult, however, to eat in restaurants for long without tasting some of them.

The cookbooks listed in the Recommended Reading section provide many recipes for preparing or using these food items. Most of the items can, however, be adapted to Western-style recipes.

Dashi 出し/だし

Dashi, fish stock made from *katsuobushi* and *kombu* (kelp), is used as a base for soups and dipping sauces in Japanese recipes. It also makes a readily available alternative to chicken and beef broths. The process for making *dashi* from scratch is described in most Japanese cookbooks.

Instant *dashi* is sold in bags that look like tea bags, in freeze-dried granular form, and as a condensed liquid. The flavors of different products vary considerably. The bags are packaged in boxes of varying sizes, some flat and some looking very much like boxes of tea bags. The most common brand of freeze-dried *dashi* is ほんだし *hondashi,* sold in a 65-gram (2-oz.) dark brown glass jar with a red lid. Use 1 scant teaspoon of this product for 1 cup of water at first, and then adjust amounts to taste. Liquid instant *dashi* comes in glass bottles. Use $\frac{1}{2}$ teaspoon for 1 cup water at first, and then adjust amounts.

Fish Paste 練りもの *nerimono*

Both food markets and food sections of department stores sell many items of food in different shapes, all stored near one another in the refrigerated case. Some of these foods look like pink or white quonset huts, others like toasted white hot dogs with holes running down the center. Still others are round balls or flat white rectangles or amorphous golden blobs with pieces of food sticking out at odd angles. All of these are forms of fish paste, usually made from ground squid and shark. The consistency and shape vary more than the taste. Fish paste is already cooked and can be served cold as appetizers, warm from the oven, or cooked in soup. Some varieties may contain sodium nitrate (a preservative) and/or hydrogen peroxide (a bleaching agent), but these chemicals may not be listed on labels.

Some common varieties of fish paste are found in most markets. *Chikuwa* ちくわ, a white and slightly toasted cylinder the size of a hot dog, has a hole running down the center. *Hampen* はんぺん is a white square, somewhat like a dumpling in consistency. *Satsuma-age* さつまあげ is a fried form, golden in color. It often contains visible pieces of seafood and vegetables. *Kamaboko* かまぼこ comes in many varieties, the most common being the one that looks like a pink or white quonset hut, 10 centimeters (4 in.) long, sold on a slab of wood. There is also a toasted form and snack varieties mixed with bits of cheese or *nori* (laver). The word *kamaboko* is sometimes used as the generic name for all fish paste.

Fu ふ

Fu is wheat gluten, either dry (called simply *fu* ふ) or fresh (生ふ *namafu*). Some dried *fu* looks like decorative croutons; when examined closely, all dried *fu* looks like dried bread. Dried *fu* is sold unrefrigerated, *namafu* in the refrigerator case. Dried *fu* is very hard and should be soaked in water and squeezed out before being used. *Fu* is used in soups and in sukiyaki and other dishes cooked at the table.

Konnyaku こんにゃく

Konnyaku, sometimes called "devil's tongue jelly" after the devil's tongue plant from which it is made, comes in several forms: rectangular blocks, small balls, fat and short "noodles," and spaghetti-like strings (白滝/しらたき *shirataki*). Each of these forms is usually sold in clear plastic bags in the refrigerated case of the market. *Konnyaku* is translucent green, gray, or brown in color, has the consistency of hard gelatin, and has no flavor of its own. Served in such cook-at-the-table dishes as sukiyaki, *konnyaku* absorbs the flavors of the ingredients with which it is cooked. A scant half cup of *konnyaku* contains only 10 calories.

Miso 味噌/みそ

Miso is a thick sauce-like food made by steaming, crushing, and fermenting soybeans either alone, to make *mame-miso* 豆みそ or in combination with rice (米みそ *komemiso*) or barley (麦みそ *mugimiso*). Mixtures of these forms are called *chōgō miso* 調合みそ "blended *miso*." The *himmei* 品名 line of the information panel lists one of these four words. The most common kind of *miso* available is *komemiso*.

From the standpoint of taste, there are two main kinds of *miso*. *Amamiso* 甘みそ is less salty and lighter in color (about the color of peanut butter or lighter); the lightest variety of *amamiso* is called *shiromiso* 白みそ "white miso." *Karamiso* 辛みそ is saltier, richer, and darker (from the color of peanut butter to dark brown) than *amamiso*. The respective words 甘口 *amakuchi* and 辛口 *karakuchi* appear

KATSUOBUSHI and shavings   INSTANT DASHI *(liquid; granular)*

INSTANT DASHI *(granular)*

KOMBU *(kelp)*

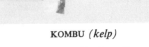

WAKAME *(fresh; dehydrated)*   HIJIKI

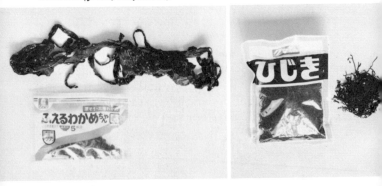

MIRIN   COOKING SAKÉ   SOY SAUCE

MISO   INSTANT MISO SOUP

NORI *(laver)*
(flavored;
unflavored)

on the front labels of some *miso* containers, as does an indication of the percentage of salt (塩 *shio*), usually from 2 to 14 percent. Some kinds of *miso* are very fine in texture, some coarse.

Miso is packaged in clear plastic bags and tubs. It will keep for a long time under refrigeration.

Miso is an ingredient in many traditional dishes both for its flavor and nutritional value. Its most common use is in *misoshiru,* "*miso* soup." *Miso* itself should not be boiled, or it will separate from the liquid. For this reason, it is usually added at the end of the preparation of a dish. Although *amamiso* is by itself salty, it will give foods a sweet taste.

Noodles 麺類 *menrui*

Noodles, eaten in broth or with a dipping sauce (see p. 121), warm the insides in winter and make a cooling meal in summer. Noodles are sold in clear plastic bags with the name of the kind of noodle on the front label and on the *himmei* 品名 line of the information panel. Precooked noodles and fresh uncooked noodles are sold in clear plastic bags found in the refrigerated section of the market. Precooked noodles require heating only. (See App. 4, p. 155, for instructions for cooking dried noodles and fresh uncooked noodles.)

Descriptions of the most common noodles available are given below. The first four kinds are wheat noodles, straight like spaghetti but tenderer and slightly more salty.

Udon うどん are long thick noodles, either round or square in cross section. They are served in hot soups and sometimes in dishes cooked at the table such as sukiyaki. *Udon* in *dashi* broth are sold at many fast-food counters.

Kishimen きしめん are similar in taste to, but flatter than, *udon*. They are served in dishes cooked at the table, and can also be used in gratin dishes, casseroles, and in winter soups. They will not become soggy when cooked for a long time, as *udon* will.

Hiyamugi ひやむぎ are the size of (and a good substitute for) standard spaghetti. They are served chilled and with a dipping sauce as part of a summer meal.

Sōmen そうめん are noodles as fine as vermicelli. They are usually sold in strands shorter than those of the other noodles, and come in white, pink, green, and yellow. Like *hiyamugi,* they are eaten cold in summer. They can also be used in soup.

Soba そば, brown noodles with a firm texture, are made from buckwheat flour. They are most often served at room temperature with a dipping sauce, although they may be served in hot soups as well. In restaurants a *soba* meal often includes tempura.

Chinese noodles 中華そば *Chūka soba* are made from wheat, but are usually yellowish in color and twisted or curved rather than straight. Perhaps the most popular Chinese noodle is *rāmen* ラーメン, the ingredient of a Chinese soup by the same name served in many small restaurants. In food markets, the noodles are sold dried in plastic bags. *Yakisoba* 焼そば/やきそば (not a buckwheat noodle) are sold either dried or precooked, the latter type refrigerated and coated with oil. These noodles are stir-fried with meat, vegetables, and sauce to make a dish also called *yakisoba*.

KAMABOKO

CHIKUWA

HAMPEN

SATSUMA-AGE

KONNYAKU

SHIRATAKI

SOBA and SŌMEN *(dried)*   FU *(dried)*

Saké 酒 *sake*

Saké, or *nihonshu* 日本酒, is dry rice wine. It is usually sold in large brown glass bottles with other liquor rather than in the food section of a market. There are three grades of saké: *tokkyūshu* 特級酒 "special class," *ikkyūshu* 一級酒 "first class," and *nikyūshu* 二級酒 "second class." Saké for cooking is called *ryōri-yō no sake* 料理用の酒. *Nikyūshu* also can be used for cooking. Saké is a common ingredient in Japanese cuisine. It is added, for example, to stir-fried vegetables and clear soup to enhance flavor.

Mirin みりん, sweet cooking saké, is commonly sold in even the smallest food markets, often stocked near the vinegar. It comes in clear bottles, varying in volume from 250 milliliters (8 fl. oz.) to 1 liter (1 qt.). Its color is light amber. *Mirin* is often used as a substitute for sugar in cooking.

Seaweed 海草 *kaisō*

Seaweed has no calories but is rich in calcium, phosphorus, vitamin A, iron, and iodine. It is usually sold dried and packaged in clear plastic. Fresh seaweed can sometimes be found in the refrigerated case in the market; it should be rinsed thoroughly before being eaten.

Hijiki ひじき, in dried form, looks somewhat like long tea leaves. After it is reconstituted, it can be cooked and eaten alone, with fried tofu, or with soybeans. It can also be added to vegetable dishes.

Kombu 昆布/こんぶ, or kelp, is the largest kind of seaweed in the market. It is flat and very dark green. *Kombu* should be wiped with a damp cloth or paper towel before being used.

There are two main varieties of *kombu*. *Dashikombu* だしこんぶ is about 10 to 15 centimeters (4 to 6 in.) wide and can be greater than 30 centimeters (1 ft.) long. It is used for making *dashi* and may also be simmered in various dishes or thrown in the rice cooker to enhance flavor. *Dashikombu* is not itself eaten, since it is very tough.

Nikombu 煮こんぶ, used for cooking in general, is not as wide as *dashikombu*. It is often sold in packages that bear the word おでん *oden,* a kind of Japanese stew. *Nikombu* can be eaten with the rest of the dish in which it is cooked.

There are several other kinds of *kombu,* such as a thinly shaved variety for clear soup and a soft form for wrapping rice balls.

Nori 海苔/のり, or laver, looks like dark green or black stiff pieces of paper. It is used primarily as an edible wrapping for rice. It also adorns rice crackers and snacks. *Nori* comes in different sizes according to the amount of rice being wrapped. The major sizes are square sheets about 20 by 20 centimeters (8 by 8 in.) and small strips about 4 by 8 centimeters ($1\frac{1}{2}$ by 3 in.).

Yakinori 焼のり is unflavored; *ajitsuke-nori* 味付のり is flavored with mirin or soy sauce. *Aonori* 青のり is *nori* in the form of small flakes. It comes plain or mixed with sesame seeds or *katsuobushi,* usually packaged in small glass jars. *Aonori* is sprinkled over rice and *yakisoba.*

Wakame わかめ, the seaweed found in *miso* soup, is sold fresh, partly dried (in long moist bunches), dried (in stiff, sticklike form), and in plastic packages in a rapidly reconstituting instant form. Packages of instant *wakame* soup in various flavors are available. Dried *wakame* is blackish green, about $\frac{1}{2}$ to 1 centimeter ($\frac{1}{4}$ to $\frac{1}{2}$ in.) in width. It reconstitutes in water in about 15 minutes, its color changing to emerald green. *Wakame* can be added uncooked to salads and stir-fried with vegetables.

Soy Sauce 醤油/しょうゆ *shōyu*

Soy sauce can be found as an ingredient in countless other sauces for special uses. Therefore, at first everything may seem to be soy sauce. Soy sauce itself, however, usually comes in either plastic or glass bottles with the Japanese word, noted above, shown clearly on the front label.

The major ingredients of soy sauce are soybeans, wheat, salt, and water. Some soy sauce also contains *mirin,* the sweet rice wine often used in cooking. If the sauce has been naturally brewed, the word 本醸造 *honjōzō* will appear on the front label and/or in the information panel.

Soy sauce is made in two main forms: *koikuchi* 濃口/こいくち "thick" and *usukuchi* うすくち "thin." *Koikuchi* soy sauce is not noticeably thick in terms of consistency, but is darker in color and richer in flavor, while *usukuchi* soy sauce is saltier. The former is the standard kind of soy sauce; the word *shōyu* alone generally refers to this kind. The thickness of the soy sauce is indicated on the *himmei* 品名 line of the information panel.

Each thickness of soy sauce is available in regular dilution, low salt (うす塩 *usu-jio;* about 13 percent less salt than in regular soy sauce), and very low salt (減塩 *gen'en;* about half the amount of salt compared to regular soy sauce). One teaspoon of regular soy sauce contains approximately $\frac{1}{4}$ teaspoon salt.

Traditional Japanese dishes such as noodles and tempura are eaten with a soy-sauce-based dipping sauce (つけ汁 *tsuke-jiru*). Recipes for such sauces can be found in Japanese cookbooks, and many prepared mixtures, either ready to use or in concentrated form, are available, in small bottles and cans. The specific use of the prepared mixtures is written clearly on the front label and in the information panel. Labels of sauces for noodles say either めんつゆ *mentsuyu* or the name of a kind of noodle (see p. 116); *mentsuyu* can be used for any noodles. Labels of tempura sauces bear the word 天ぷら *tempura*.

To determine whether a prepared sauce has to be diluted, taste a drop of the product. If the sauce tastes too strong, take a small amount and dilute it by adding an equal part of water; taste. Continue adding equal parts of water as necessary.

Most sauces for noodles can also be made into a hot or cold noodle broth (かけ汁 *kake-jiru*) into which the noodles are placed after they are cooked and drained. Broth made from a particular concentrated sauce-product usually has to be made more diluted than dipping sauce made from that product.

Dipping sauces for *sashimi* 刺身/さしみ, labeled with this word, also exist. Such sauces usually need not be diluted. *Koikuchi* soy sauce is also commonly used for *sashimi*.

Tofu 豆腐/とうふ *tōfu*

Tofu, soybean curd, has become recognized outside the Orient for its value as a high-protein, low-fat, nutritious, and economical food. It has a subtle flavor, often slightly sweet when made by a good tofu maker. Cut into cubes, it is served in soups, cooked with Chinese-style sauces, and added to sukiyaki and Chinese-style stir-fried meat or vegetable dishes. It can be used as a cool custard for a summer lunch. Its uses are limited only by the imagination. The two tofu cookbooks in the Recommended Reading section contain a large number of recipes using this food.

Plain tofu is creamy white in color and is sold in blocks about 10 by 6 by 4 centimeters (4 by $2\frac{1}{2}$ by $1\frac{1}{2}$ in.), in two consistencies. *Kinu-dōfu* 絹どうふ, *kinu-goshi* 絹ごし, or simply *kinu* 絹/きぬ "silk," is custard-like and very delicate. *Men-dōfu* 綿どうふ, or simply *momen* 木綿/もめん "cotton," is slightly more coarse and dense, and is easier to handle with chopsticks than *kinu-dōfu.*

Yaki-dōfu 焼どうふ is *men-dōfu* whose surface has been seared slightly. It comes in blocks, sometimes less thick than those of regular tofu, and is easily identifiable by the brown sear marks on its surface. *Yaki-dōfu* is easier to handle and less fragile than regular tofu, so it is often the kind used in sukiyaki and other dishes cooked at the table.

Nama-age 生揚 is deep-fried tofu *(men-dōfu)* about half the thickness of regular tofu. The outer surface is honey-colored; the inner part of the block remains soft. A deep-fried tofu that contains other ingredients, such as *hijiki,* is called *gammodoki* がんもどき or *gammo* がんも. *Gammo* is sold in about the size and shape of a small hamburger. It is best cooked in sweetened soy sauce.

Abura-age 油揚 is also a deep-fried version of tofu, but since it is thinner than *nama-age,* no soft part remains. *Abura-age* is sold in pouch form, to be stuffed with vinegared rice in making a finger-food called *inari-zushi.*

Okara おから is a yellowish fluff that is a by-product of the tofu-making process. This can be bought fresh from barrels at the neighborhood tofu shop. Fresh *okara* is most commonly sautéed with other vegetables. At supermarkets, a prepared *okara*-vegetable mix is sold.

In the supermarket, blocks of regular tofu and *yaki-dōfu* are sold refrigerated in small plastic tubs filled with liquid. Fried forms of tofu are sold refrigerated in plastic bags without liquid. The date of manufacture is prominently stamped on packages of tofu. Avoid buying tofu more than two days old or whose liquid looks yellowish. Regular tofu sold in the neighborhood tofu shop has been made that day. The shopkeeper will place the tofu in a plastic container and then a bag. It should be handled carefully as you carry it home.

TOFU (MEN and KINU)

YAKI-DŌFU   NAMA-AGE

ABURA-AGE

GAMMO

All forms of tofu spoil quickly and should therefore be kept in the refrigerator. Tofu is best eaten on the day of purchase. Before preparing and eating *nama-age* and *abura-age,* pour hot water over them to help remove the oil in which they were fried.

Tofu sold in the supermarket may contain as many as ten ingredients. One brand includes the following: soybeans, gluconic acid, calcium sulfate, magnesium chloride, coagulant, glycerine, fatty acid ester, calcium carbonate, and an anti-foaming agent. The fewest ingredients in packaged tofu are soybeans, coagulant, and a chemical to remove air bubbles. Other possible ingredients may be substances to enhance flavor, alter the texture, or increase the shelf life of the product. Tofu bought directly from a tofu maker may be the purest product. Not all tofu tastes the same, and if there is more than one tofu shop in your neighborhood, you may want to sample the flavors of each shop.

Tofu shops are working establishments, often dark inside with an abundance of water all over the floor. The tofu itself is stored in deep water-filled tubs. Stainless steel machinery in the shop makes the tofu or fries the *abura-age.* Barrels of *okara* may stand on the sidewalk outside the shop. To buy tofu from the tofu maker, ask for both the kind and the number of blocks or sheets desired:*

EXAMPLES: Please give me 1 block of *kinu-goshi*.
          Kinu-goshi o itchō kudasai.

          Please give me 1 sheet of *abura-age*.
          Abura-age o ichimai kudasai.

* See Appendix 1 (pp. 144, 145) for numbers used when asking for tofu.

19 · HOUSEHOLD NEEDS:
Non-Edibles

Some of the large supermarket chains package their own brands of household products at prices slightly lower than those of name brands. Also, no-brand (無印 *mujirushi*) products are available at even greater savings.

The information panel of non-edible products contains categories different from those found on food products. The most common categories are listed below; some products carry other categories as well, and some labels list the categories in an order different from that given below. It is common to see this information written horizontally across the back label rather than in a separate box as on food labels.

品名   *himmei,* product (generic) name (see p. 33)

成分   *seibun,* formula (ingredients, and sometimes the percentage of each contained)

液性   *ekisei,* pH (for liquid products only: usually either 弱アルカリ性 *jaku-arukari-sei,* "weak alkali," or 中性 *chūsei,* "neutral")

用途   *yōto,* uses

Information indicating whether a product is in liquid form (液体 *ekitai*), granular (粒 *tsubu*), or powdered (粉 *kona*) does not usually appear in the information panel (unless the pH happens to be stated).

The headings of the sections below correspond in most cases to the generic name of the product.

← お使いになる前に必ずお読みください。

■酸素系の衛生漂白剤ですから、いやなニオイがなく、手におだやかでヌルヌルしません. 安心してお使いいただけます.

シミ・ヨゴレを落とす ■つけておくだけで、茶わん・きゅうすなどの茶しぶや黒ずみ、ふきん・おしぼりなどのシミや黄ばみもきれいに落とします.

バイキン・ニオイを除く ■ふきん・まな板・ゴミ入れなどのバイキンやニオイを除き、衛生的に仕上げます.

● 色・柄物のふきん・おしぼりにも使えます. ●ぬるめのお湯（約40℃）をお使いください.
● 食器などは、浸したあとスポンジなどで軽く洗い流してください.

家庭用品品質表示法に基づく表示		キャップ1杯は…約15g
●品名/漂白剤	●成分/過炭酸ナトリウム（酸素系）、界面活性剤、炭酸塩	
●液性/弱アルカリ性	●正味量/260g	

使用方法	用途	●ふきん、おしぼりの漂白と除菌・除臭 ●冷蔵庫、食器棚の除菌・除臭 ●まな板、食器、ボール、洗浄用具、ゴミ入れ、ザルの漂白と除菌・除臭 ●茶しぶの漂白 ●哺乳びんの除菌・除臭
	標準使用量	●2ℓの水に8g（キャップ約半分）
	使い方	●よく溶かし、30分ぐらい（汚れのひどいときは少し長めに）浸したあと水ですすぎます. 浸せないものは、液に浸した布をしぼってふいたあと水ぶきします.
	使えるもの	●白物、色物、柄物のせんい製品（木綿、麻、化学せんい）●プラスチック製品 ●木・竹製品 ●陶器 ●ガラス器
	使えないもの	●毛、絹のせんい製品 ●水や洗剤で色が出るもの ●含金属染料で染めたもの ●金属製の容器、用具 ●漆器
		●試し方…湯に溶かした濃いめの液を目立たない部分につけて5分ほどおき、変色するものや、白布をあててもんで色が移るものには使わないでください. ●冷水よりも温水の方が早く効果が出ます. ●せんい自体が変質して黄ばんだものは、漂白剤でも元に戻りません.

使用上の注意	●幼児の手が届く所に置かないでください. ●熱湯では使わないでください. ●粉が皮ふについたときは、水で洗い流してください. ●万一飲みこんだときは、すぐ吐かせ、牛乳か生卵を飲ませてください. 目に入ったときは、すぐ水でじゅうぶん洗い流してください. どちらの場合もすぐ処置したうえ、医師にみてもらってください. ●直射日光を避け、高温の所に置かないでください.

花王石鹸株式会社　〒103東京都中央区日本橋茅場町1-14-10
☎03(665)6211　Ⓢ

家庭用品品質表示法に基づく表示	
品　名	洗たく用合成洗剤
成　分	界面活性剤(25%) 直鎖アルキルベンゼン系 高級アルコール系（陰イオン） りん酸塩(P₂O₅として0%) 硫酸塩、けい酸塩 アルミノけい酸塩 けい光剤配合
液　性	弱アルカリ性
用　途	麻・木綿・化学繊維用
正　味　量	500g
標準使用量	水30ℓに対して40g（200mℓのコップで約7分目）

品質表示	
品名	台所用合成洗剤
成分	界面活性剤（1%） りん酸塩 P_2O_5 として（12%） けい酸塩・炭酸塩 漂白剤配合
液性	アルカリ性
用途	食器用（全自動食器洗い機用）
正味量	1kg
標準使用量	水5ℓに対して10g（料理用大さじ約一杯）

Information panels for
kitchen-use bleach,
laundry and dish detergents.

Aluminum Foil アルミニューム ホイル *aruminyūmu hoiru*

Foil is packaged in long cardboard boxes similar to those found abroad. The words "foil" or "cooking foil" are often written in English on the box. The length of the roll is usually indicated in meters (m.).

Anti-Static Spray

Anti-static spray for clothing comes in small aerosol cans. Labels often show pictures of clothing being sprayed. The words 衣類の静電気を防ぐ *irui no seidenki o fusegu* or 衣類の静電気防止に *irui no seidenki bōshi ni,* "to prevent clothing static," usually appear somewhere on the labels of these products.

Bags

Bags for food storage (ポリ袋 *pori-bukuro*) are often sold in large plastic bags or in boxes similar in shape to those used for plastic wrap. Pictures on the labels indicate the intended use. Labels of freezer bags are marked with the word 冷凍用 *reitō-yō,* "freezer use." Small paper bags for carrying lunches are rare.*

Garbage bags (ゴミ袋 *gomi-bukuro*) come in both plastic and heavy paper. The size in centimeters (cm.), the capacity in liters (1. or リットル *rittoru*), and the number of bags included (枚 *mai*) may appear on the label.

Bathroom Cleaner 浴室用洗浄剤 *yokushitsu-yō senjōzai*

Bathroom cleaners, usually liquids, are designed either

* One shop—located in a side alley in the retail section of the Tsukiji Central Market in Tokyo (near Tsukiji Station on the Hibiya subway line)—sells several sizes of paper bags in quantities of 100 at reasonable prices. The shop can be identified by the huge quantities of white plastic bags and chopsticks displayed in front.

to prevent or remove mildew. They are basically the same in formula as kitchen mildew removers, discussed below under "Household Detergents." They come in plastic bottles that look like dish detergent containers. Illustrations on the label may indicate that rubber gloves should be worn.

Bleach 漂白剤 *hyōhakuzai*

Two kinds of bleaches are available: kitchen bleaches for cleaning utensils and laundry bleaches for washing clothes. Both bleaches come in powdered and liquid forms.

The *himmei* 品名 line of the information panel does not distinguish between powdered and liquid bleaches. The powdered form usually comes in cylindrical, wide-mouthed containers, while liquid bleaches come in bottle-shaped containers. To make sure which form of bleach a certain product is, simply shake the container.

Kitchen and laundry bleaches also are not distinguished on the *himmei* line. Kitchen bleaches are packaged in containers of various colors. Laundry bleaches usually come in light blue opaque containers. Front labels of the former may say キッチン *kitchin,* "kitchen," in large letters, and the *yōto* 用途 line of the information panel will include the word 食器 *shokki,* "tableware." The *yōto* line of laundry bleaches will say something like 洗たくのときに *sentaku no toki ni,* "when laundering." The characters 色物用 *iromono-yō* appear on boxes of powdered bleach that is safe for colors.

Liquid bleaches usually contain chlorine (次亜塩素酸 ナトリウム *jia-ensosan natoryūmu*); powdered ones usually do not.

Cleanser クレンザー *kurenzā*

Powdered cleansers come in the typical cylindrical cardboard canisters or in cylindrical plastic containers. Liquid cleansers come in opaque plastic bottles flattened front to back. The *seibun* 成分 line of the information panel lists the percentage of abrasives (けんま剤 *kemmazai*) and surfactants (detergent) (界面活性剤 *kaimenkasseizai*) in the product. Liquid cleansers range between 50 and 53 percent abrasives, imported powder between 69 and 70 percent, and domestic powder between 87 and 90 percent. The high-abrasive domestic powders are often strong enough to remove the enamel surface from sinks.

Dish Detergent 台所用合成洗剤 *daidokoro-yō gōseisenzai*

Most dish detergents are in liquid form. The *seibun* 成分 line of the information panel indicates the percentage of detergent (界面活性剤 *kaimenkasseizai*), usually between 17 and 32 percent. Some dish detergents are safe enough for washing vegetables and fruit. Look on the *yōto* 用途 line of the information panel for the words 野菜 *yasai,* "vegetables," and 果物 *kudamono,* "fruit."

Most liquid dish detergents are packaged in clear, green, or yellow plastic bottles. A green or yellow liquid shows through the clear ones. Sizes range from 350 to 2,150 milliliters (12 fl. oz. to $2\frac{1}{3}$ qt.).

A solid block of dish detergent with the brand name パロン *paron* is sold in plastic containers that look like margarine tubs. This product is highly concentrated, equivalent to 600 milliliters (20 fl. oz.) of liquid detergent, according to the label. It is used by applying a wet sponge to the soap.

Dishwasher Detergent

Most automatic dishwasher detergents sold in Japan are imported (with labels in English), but there is at least one domestic product. For the latter, only the word 合成洗剤 *gōseisenzai,* "detergent," may appear on the *himmei* 品名 line; look for the word 全自動食器洗い機 *zenjidō shokki araiki,* "automatic dishwasher," on the *yōto* 用途 line.

Drain Cleaner 排水パイプ用洗浄剤 *haisuipaipu-yō senjōzai*

Drain cleaners are packaged in plastic bottles or in cylindrical containers like kitchen cleansers; pictures of plumbing pipes are on the labels. Instructions on the back label are usually accompanied by pictures indicating the procedure for use. The two most important words needed to read the instructions are カップ *kappu,* "cup" and 分 *fun,* "minute." (See App. 2 regarding the size of a Japanese cup measure.) Many of these products are for use with metal pipes only. Therefore, when in doubt, check with the owner or manager of your residence if drain problems arise.

Fabric Softener 柔軟仕上げ剤 *jūnan shiagezai*

Liquid fabric softeners, added to the washing process, are packaged in pink or blue opaque bottles. Tissue fabric softeners, to be added to the dryer (like Cling Free or Bounce), are packaged in boxes.

Household Detergent 住宅用洗剤 *jūtaku-yō senzai*
住宅用合成洗剤 *jūtaku-yō gōseisenzai*

The above names are broad terms for glass cleaners, kitchen mildew removers, and general purpose detergents. The word 家具用 *kagu-yō,* "for furniture," may be included in the name. Pictures on the label, rather than the information panel, are the best guide to the specific use of the product. Containers for general purpose detergents are usually a shade of green, yellow, or blue, and have a red or orange cap. Glass cleaners are usually packaged in white, semi-

DISH DETERGENT

BLEACH *(powder; liquid)*

CLEANSERS *(liquid)*

CLEANSER *(powder)*

MILDEW CLEANER
(for kitchen)

GLASS CLEANER

HOUSEHOLD DETERGENTS

DRAIN-PIPE CLEANER

TILE CLEANER

BATH CLEANER

TOILET CLEANER

DRAIN-PIPE CLEANER
(for toilet)

DEODORANT/CLEANING FLUID
(for toilet tank)

opaque bottles with blue liquid showing through. Some bottles have hand sprays attached to the caps. Some glass cleaners come in aerosol cans. Look for the word ガラス *garasu,* "glass," on the label. Kitchen mildew cleaner labels usually have pictures of kitchen sinks and the word カビ *kabi,* "mildew," on them.

Laundry Detergent 合成洗剤系洗たく剤 *gōseisenzai-kei sentakuzai*
洗濯用合成洗剤 *sentaku-yō gōseisenzai*

Laundry detergents come in liquid and powdered form for general laundry use and for specific cleaning tasks such as woolens and silks, canvas shoes, shirt collars, and the like. The *himmei* 品名 line of the information panel does not usually distinguish among these different detergents, but the specific use can be determined from other information, discussed below. The *seibun* 成分 line states the percentage of detergent (界面活性剤 *kaimenkasseizai*) in the product.

General laundry detergent. Liquid detergent comes in plastic containers, powdered detergent in boxes. The package designs for both are similar to those of detergents sold in the West. Very small containers of some brands of liquid detergent have special caps for applying the detergent directly to stains before washing.

The concentration of detergent for liquid products usually ranges from 30 to 49 percent, and that for powder from 15 to 27 percent. The higher the percentage of detergent, the greater the likelihood that the product will fade colored clothes.

Canvas shoes. Pictures of shoes appear on the front label of containers of this detergent. Containers are smaller than those of general laundry detergents.

LAUNDRY DETERGENTS *(powder; liquid)*

DETERGENT
(for silks, woolens)

FABRIC SOFTENER
(liquid)

LAUNDRY STARCH *(liquid; spray)*

ANTI-STATIC SPRAY

BLEACH
(for colored fabrics)

Shirt collars. Prewash sprays for shirt collars come in aerosol cans with pictures of shirts on the labels.

Silks and woolens. These detergents are usually sold in liquid form in containers smaller than those of general laundry detergents. Look for the character 毛 *ke,* "wool," on the *yōto* 用途 line of the information panel. (This character will not appear on the *yōto* line of general laundry-detergent labels.)

Laundry Starch 洗濯糊 *sentaku nori*

Laundry starch comes powdered (in boxes), in liquid form (in plastic containers), and in aerosol cans. Instructions for dissolving the powdered and liquid forms in water are included on the back label. It is safest to consult with a person who reads the language to get the proportions and times correct.

Starch in aerosol cans is sprayed on garments when they are ironed. All spray starches have pictures of irons on the labels.

Paper Napkins 紙ナプキン *kami napukin*

Paper napkins come in small quantities, about 25 to 40 to a package, wrapped in clear plastic. They are available in party-goods stores and in some food markets. An alternative to paper napkins is *oshibori,* those terrycloth hand-towels given to customers at many restaurants. *Oshibori* are available at reasonable prices at restaurant supply stores. They can be tossed into the laundry and reused without being ironed.

Paper Towels ペーパー タオル *pēpā taoru*

Paper towels are available either in the usual rolls, two rolls to a package, or in flat form. Prewetted paper towels

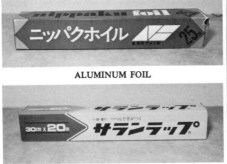

ALUMINUM FOIL

PLASTIC WRAP

**PRE-WETTED
PAPER TOWELS**

REFRIGERATOR DEODORIZER

DEHUMIDIFIER CRYSTALS
(no-brand)

BATH SALTS
Basu Kurin (not a bath cleaner)
Shawa Shawa (not for showers)

**DISPOSABLE
DUSTING PAPER**

are also available, most commonly in individual packets or in plastic containers.

Plastic Wrap ラップ フィルム *rappu firumu*

Plastic wrap comes in boxes similar to those found abroad. The length of the roll is indicated in meters (m.).

Tissues ティシュー *tishū*

Most tissues are packaged in the usual cardboard boxes. Stores often run specials in which several boxes can be bought at a substantially lower price per box. Small plastic packets of tissues for handbag and pocket use are sold in most supermarkets, but you can maintain a permanent free supply of these by walking past banks on a regular basis.

Toilet Cleaner トイレット用洗浄剤 *toiretto-yō senjōzai*
Toilet Deodorant Liquid トイレ消臭液 *toire shōshū-eki*

Two kinds of toilet-cleaning products are sold: liquid detergents to be applied directly to the toilet bowl for one-time cleaning and those to be put in the water reservoir for continuous cleaning and/or deodorizing. All products intended for water reservoirs have pictures on their labels indicating the proper placement of the product. The actual space in some reservoirs is limited, so it is best to check the size of the reservoir before buying the deodorizer.

In addition to the above, solid and spray room-deodorizers are available.

Toilet Paper トイレット ペーパー *toiretto pēpā*
トイレット ティシュー *toiretto tishū*

Packaged in plastic wrapping containing 4, 6, or more rolls, this product looks like those sold abroad. The cheaper brands may have a coarse texture.

✕ APPENDIXES

1. COUNTING IN JAPANESE

Japanese has two sets of words for counting from 1 to 10, one set native to Japanese, the other adopted from Chinese. Beyond 10, only the Chinese-derived numbers are used (Table 5, p. 142).

To ask for a certain number of most objects, the native Japanese numbers can be used for up to 10 of the objects, the Chinese-derived numbers for 11 and above. The basic word order in such a request is "object+*o*+number+*kudasai* [please give me]."

EXAMPLES: Please give me 2 of those.
Sore o futatsu kudasai.

Please give me 5 fish.
Sakana o itsutsu kudasai.

Please give me 12.
Jū-ni kudasai.

The word for "How many?" is *ikutsu*.

The above will be understood in most cases and is the suggested wording for beginners. However, the proper way to count objects is to attach to the number a suffix, or "counter," that denotes the shape or nature of the object. (This is similar to the English "1 *slice* of bread," "3 *sticks* of butter," etc.) Some counters go with the native Japanese numbers (from which the *-tsu* is deleted), and some with the Chinese-derived numbers. Beyond 10 of anything, the Chinese numbers have to be used with the counters. If there is no clear counter for a certain object, the numbers alone, as in the examples above, are perfectly correct.

Several of the more important counters are given below. For each counter, the words for 1 to 10 of the type of object are listed. Below these, the word for "how many?" appropriate

TABLE 5: Japanese Numbers

Native Japanese Numbers	Chinese-derived Numbers	
1–10	**1–10**	**Tens**
1 hitotsu 一つ	ichi 一(壱)	jū 十
2 futatsu 二つ	ni 二(弐)	nijū 二十
3 mittsu 三つ	san 三(参)	sanjū 三十
4 yottsu 四つ	shi *or* yon (yo) 四	yonjū (shijū)
5 itsutsu 五つ	go 五	gojū
6 muttsu 六つ	roku 六	rokujū
7 nanatsu 七つ	shichi *or* nana 七	nanajū (shichijū)
8 yattsu 八つ	hachi 八	hachijū
9 kokonotsu 九つ	kyū *or* ku 九	kyūjū (kujū)
10 tō 十	jū 十(拾)	

Note: The words in parentheses are less common alternate forms. The kanji in parentheses are sometimes used on price signs in neighborhood shops.

EXAMPLES: 11 jū-ichi 十一
15 jū-go 十五

to the counter is given. (As a rule, for counters that take the Japanese numbers, "how many?" is expressed by *iku-*+counter; for the counters which attach to the Chinese-derived numbers, "how many?" is *nan-*+counter. The general word *ikutsu* can safely be used for "how many?" in most cases.) A sample sentence is shown last. Please note that when alternate forms for a number exist (e.g., *shi, yon,* or *yo* for 4), only one of these may be correct for a given counter. Note also that when the number and counter are connected, a sound change sometimes takes place (e.g., *ichi*+*hon*=*ippon*).*

---

* In the list on page 26, those suffixes preceded by *ichi* can take any of the Chinese-derived numbers, and those preceded by *hito* can take the other Japanese numbers.

Chinese-derived Numbers *(cont'd)*		
Hundreds	Thousands	Ten Thousands
hyaku 百	sen 千 *or* issen 一千	ichiman 一万 (一萬)
nihyaku 二百	nisen 二千	niman 二万
sambyaku 三百	sanzen 三千	samman 三万
yonhyaku	yonsen	yomman
gohyaku	gosen	goman
roppyaku	rokusen	rokuman
nanahyaku	nanasen	nanaman
happyaku	hassen	hachiman
kyūhyaku	kyūsen	kyūman
		jūman

28   nijū-hachi 二十八
36   sanjū-roku 三十六
250   nihyaku-gojū 二百五十
675   roppyaku-nanajū-go 六百七十五
2,430   nisen-yonhyaku-sanjū 二千四百三十
23,000   niman-sanzen 二万三千

-**Kire** 切 is used with the native Japanese numbers (except 9) to count flat cuts of meat (chops), fish fillets, and the like.

1 *hito-kire*	5 *itsu-kire*	8 *ya-kire*
2 *futa-kire*	6 *mu-kire*	9 *kyū-kire*
3 *mi-kire*	7 *nana-kire*	10 *to-kire*
4 *yo-kire*		

How many? *iku-kire* or *ikutsu*

EXAMPLES: Please give me 3 fillets of cod.
Tara o mi-kire kudasai.

Please give me 2 fillets of pork tenderloin.
Buta no hire o futakire kudasai.

-Chō 丁 is used with the Chinese-derived numbers to count blocks of such items as tofu.

1	*itchō*	5	*go-chō*	8	*hatchō*
2	*ni-chō*	6	*roku-chō*	9	*kyū-chō*
3	*san-chō*	7	*nana-chō*	10	*jutchō/jitchō*
4	*yon-chō*				

How many? *nan-chō* or *ikutsu*

EXAMPLE: Please give me 3 blocks of *momen* tofu.
Momen o san-chō kudasai.

-Hiki 匹 is used with the Chinese-derived numbers to count whole fish.

1	*ippiki*	5	*go-hiki*	8	*happiki*
2	*ni-hiki*	6	*roppiki*	9	*kyū-hiki*
3	*sambiki*	7	*nana-hiki*	10	*juppiki/jippiki*
4	*yon-hiki*				

How many? *nambiki* or *ikutsu*

EXAMPLE: Please give me 2 fish.
Sakana o ni-hiki kudasai.

-Hon 本 is used with the Chinese-derived numbers to count long objects, such as chicken legs, carrots, and bottles.

1	*ippon*	5	*go-hon*	8	*hachi-hon/happon*
2	*ni-hon*	6	*roppon*	9	*kyū-hon*
3	*sambon*	7	*nana-hon*	10	*juppon/jippon*
4	*yon-hon*				

How many? *nambon* or *ikutsu*

EXAMPLE: Please give me 4 (chicken) legs.
Momo o yon-hon kudasai.

-Ko 個 is used with the Chinese-derived numbers to count various objects—grapefruit, tomatoes, dinner rolls, etc. This suffix can be used for many compact objects.

1	*ikko*	5	*go-ko*
2	*ni-ko*	6	*rokko*
3	*san-ko*	7	*nana-ko*
4	*yon-ko*		

8	*hachi-ko/hakko*
9	*kyū-ko*
10	*jukko/jikko*

How many? *nan-ko* or *ikutsu*

EXAMPLE: Please give me 6 tomatoes.
  Tomato o rokko kudasai.

-Mai 枚 is used with the Chinese-derived numbers to count flat, sheet-like objects, such as thin slices of meat and *abura-age*.

1	*ichi-mai*	5	*go-mai*	8	*hachi-mai*
2	*ni-mai*	6	*roku-mai*	9	*kyū-mai*
3	*sammai*	7	*nana-mai*	10	*jū-mai*
4	*yommai*				

How many? *nammai* or *ikutsu*

EXAMPLE: Please give me 5 pieces of *abura-age*.
  Abura-age o go-mai kudasai.

-Wa 羽 is used with the Chinese-derived numbers to count whole chickens, ducks, etc.

1	*ichi-wa*	5	*go-wa*	8	*hachi-wa*
2	*ni-wa*	6	*roku-wa·*	9	*kyū-wa*
3	*samba*	7	*nana-wa*	10	*juppa/jippa*
4	*yon-wa*				

How many? *namba* or *ikutsu*

EXAMPLE: Please give me 1 (whole) chicken.
  Tori o ichi-wa kudasai.

Yen

The word for "yen," *en* (円 or ¥), functions as a counter when it is used with numbers. It is attached to the Chinese-derived numbers. To express amounts of yen other than those shown below, build up the numbers in the manner shown in Table 5 (p. 142).

1	*ichi en*	6	*roku en*	100	*hyaku en*
2	*ni en*	7	*shichi en/nana en*	1,000	*sen en*
3	*san en*	8	*hachi en*	10,000	*ichiman en*
4	*yo en*	9	*kyū en*		
5	*go en*	10	*jū en*		

How much? *ikura*

EXAMPLES: How much is this?
Kore wa ikura desu ka?
It's 94 yen.
Kyūjū-yo en desu.

Metric Units

The words for gram, kilogram, liter, and milliliter are preceded by the Chinese-derived numbers.

100 grams   *hyaku guramu*
2 kilograms   *ni kiroguramu/ni kiro*
500 milliliters   *gohyaku miriritoru*
3 liters   *san rittoru*
How many? *nan-guramu, nan-rittoru,* etc.

EXAMPLES: Please give me 500 grams of ground meat.
Hikiniku o gohyaku guramu kudasai.

2. WEIGHTS AND MEASURES

Japan uses the metric system for measurements of weight, volume, bulk, and temperature. If you come from a country that does not use the metric system, the differences in measurement will affect the following in particular:

• Cookbooks may give oven temperatures in degrees Fahrenheit (°F) while cooking directions on labels of Japanese products will give oven temperatures in degrees centigrade (°C; also called Celsius). The oven, on the other hand, may indicate temperatures in one of these scales or in some altogether different system depending on where the appliance was made.

• Cooking directions on a Japanese food label, if they involve volume, will be given in Japanese cups (or metric units), which differ in capacity from cooking-cups used in the English-speaking world.

The tables in this Appendix indicate equivalents between standard weights and measures used in the United States, Canada, Australia, Great Britain, and Japan. The tables are intended to be useful both for converting metric measurements on labels and for reading cooking instructions and recipes. The following information may be of particular use:

• Measuring teaspoons and tablespoons are the same in the United States, Canada, Great Britain, and Japan. The French *cuillère à café* is equal to the Japanese teaspoon; the *cuillère à soupe* is equal to the Japanese tablespoon.

• In the metric system, weight is given in grams (g.) and kilograms (kg.); liquid volume in milliliters (ml.) and liters (l.); and capacity or bulk in cubic centimeters (cc.).

• Milliliters and cubic centimeters are virtually the same in practice and can be used interchangeably for any cooking directions. The standard cup-measures sold in Japan contain

200 cubic centimeters, usually marked in 50-cc. lines and sometimes also in fractions of a cup. When a recipe calls for a certain number of milliliters of some ingredient, simply measure out that number of cubic centimeters.

The equivalents most often used are:

$$1 \text{ kg.} = 2 \text{ lb. } 3 \text{ oz.}$$
$$100 \text{ g.} = \tfrac{1}{5} \text{ lb. (approx.)}$$
$$1 \text{ lb.} = 454 \text{ g.}$$
1 Japanese cup = $\tfrac{4}{5}$ U.S./Canadian/Australian-breakfast cup
1 U.S./Canadian/Australian-breakfast cup = 237 cc. (ml.)

Weight

TABLE 6: English to Metric Weights

English	Metric
1 oz.	28 g.
4 oz.	113 g.
8 oz.	227 g.
12 oz.	340 g.
16 oz. (= 1 1b.)	454 g.

TABLE 7: Metric to English Weights

Metric	English
100 g.	$3\tfrac{1}{2}$ oz.
200 g.	7 oz.
500 g.	1 1b. $1\tfrac{1}{2}$ oz.
1,000 g. (= 1 kg.)	2 1b. 3 oz.

Volume

In the tables in this section, the designation "American" is used for convenience to refer to U.S., Canadian, and Australian measures, which are equivalent, except as noted.

Table 8 shows what Japanese or metric measures to use if the instructions in your cookbook or recipe are given in terms of

U.S., Canadian, or Australian units and you have only Japanese measuring equipment available. The equivalents shown are close approximates sufficient for most cooking purposes. (The last two figures of the last column give close to exact equivalents.)

The Australian tablespoon is about $1\frac{1}{2}$ times larger than U.S./Canadian tablespoon, and the Australian teaspoon slightly smaller than the U.S./Canadian teaspoon. (The first two rows of the Table are therefore correct for only the U.S./Canadian teaspoon and tablespoon.)

TABLE 8: American to Japanese and Metric Measures

American	Japanese	Metric
1 teaspoon	1 teaspoon	5 cc. (ml.)
1 Tablespoon	1 Tablespoon	15 cc.
1 fluid oz.	2 T.	30 cc.
$\frac{1}{4}$ cup	$\frac{3}{10}$ cup	60 cc.
$\frac{1}{3}$ c.	$\frac{2}{5}$ c.	80 cc.
$\frac{1}{2}$ c.	$\frac{3}{5}$ c.	120 cc.
$\frac{2}{3}$ c.	$\frac{4}{5}$ c.	160 cc.
$\frac{3}{4}$ c.	$\frac{9}{10}$ c.	180 cc.
1 c.	$1\frac{1}{5}$ c.	240 cc.
1 pint	$2\frac{1}{3}$ c.	473 cc.
1 quart	$4\frac{3}{4}$ c.	946 cc.

Table 9 (p. 150) shows what Japanese or metric measures to use if the instructions in your cookbook or recipe are given in terms of British Imperial units and you have only Japanese measuring equipment available. The cup measure is no longer in standard use in Great Britain, but the equivalent for it is given here.

Table 10 (p. 150) shows what American and British measures to use if the instructions on a label or in a cookbook are given in terms of Japanese and/or metric units and you have only American or British measuring equipment available. The equivalents between the Japanese and metric units are exact as shown here. (See p. 149 regarding the Australian teaspoon and tablespoon.)

TABLE 9: British Imperial to Japanese and Metric Measures

British	Japanese	Metric
1 teaspoon	1 teaspoon	5 cc. (ml.)
1 Tablespoon	1 Tablespoon	15 cc.
1 fluid oz.	2 T.	28 cc.
5 fl. oz. ($\frac{1}{2}$ cup)	$\frac{7}{10}$ cup	142 cc.
10 fl. oz. (1 c.)	$1\frac{2}{5}$ c.	284 cc.
1 pint	$2\frac{4}{5}$ c.	568 cc.
1 quart	$5\frac{7}{10}$ c.	1,136 cc.

TABLE 10: Japanese and Metric to
American and British Imperial Measures

Japanese and Metric		American	British
1 teaspoon	= 5 cc. (ml.)	1 teaspoon	1 teaspoon
1 Tablespoon	= 15 cc.	1 Tablespoon	1 Tablespoon
$\frac{1}{4}$ cup	= 50 cc.	$\frac{1}{5}$ cup	2$^-$ fl. oz.
$\frac{1}{2}$ c.	= 100 cc.	$\frac{2}{5}$ c. (3$\frac{1}{2}$ fl. oz.)	3$\frac{1}{2}$ fl. oz.
$\frac{3}{4}$ c.	= 150 cc.	$\frac{3}{5}$ c. (5 fl. oz.)	$\frac{1}{4}$+ pt. (5$^+$ fl. oz.)
1 c.	= 200 cc.	$\frac{4}{5}$ c. (7 fl. oz.)	$\frac{1}{3}$+ pt. (7 fl. oz.)
$1\frac{1}{2}$ c.	= 300 cc.	$1\frac{1}{4}$ c. (10 fl. oz.)	$\frac{1}{2}$+ pt. (10$\frac{1}{2}$ fl. oz.)
2 c.	= 400 cc.	$1\frac{2}{3}$ c. (13$\frac{1}{2}$ fl. oz.)	$\frac{2}{3}$ pt. (14 fl. oz.)
$2\frac{1}{2}$ c.	= 500 cc.	2$^+$ c. (17 fl. oz.)	$\frac{7}{8}$ pt. (18 fl. oz.)
5 c.	=1,000 cc. (1 lit.)	$4\frac{1}{4}$ c. (34 fl. oz.)	$1\frac{3}{4}$ pt. (35 fl. oz.)

Note: The designations $^-$ and $^+$ refer to "scant" and "slightly over," respectively.

Temperature

TABLE 11: Common Temperatures

	Fahrenheit (°F)	Centigrade (°C)
Freezer	0	−18
Freezing Point	32	0
Refrigerator	40	4
Room Temperature	65–70	17–21
Boiling Point	212	100

TABLE 12: Oven Temperatures

Fahrenheit (°F)	Centigrade (°C)	French ranges	British ranges (Gas mark)
200	93	#1	
225	107	#2	#$\frac{1}{4}$
250	121	low #3	#$\frac{1}{2}$
275	135	mid #3	#1
300	149	high #3	#2
325	163	mid #4	#3
350	177	high #4	#4
375	190	low #5	#5
400	205	mid #5	#6
425	218	low #6	#7
450	232	mid #6	#8
475	246	high #6	#9
500	260	#7	
525	274	#8	
550	288	#9	

3. TERMS USED IN COOKING INSTRUCTIONS

The back labels of many products come complete with pictures and step-by-step instructions for preparation, each step prefixed by a number. The section is usually headed by the terms 調理方法 *chōri hōhō*, "method of preparation," or 作り方 *tsukuri-kata*, "cooking instructions."

Listed below are some words that appear in cooking instructions. A judicious examination of the words and pictures on the label may tell you all you need to know.

分	*fun*, minutes
カップ	*kappu*, cup (see App. 2)
滴	*teki*, drop
茶さじ	*chasaji*, teaspoon
小さじ	*kosaji*, teaspoon
大さじ	*ōsaji*, tablespoon
沸かす	*wakasu*, to boil
解く/解かす	*toku/tokasu*, to dissolve, to beat (an egg)
溶かす	*tokasu*, to melt; to dissolve
入れる	*ireru*, to put in
焼く	*yaku*, to roast, bake, grill, toast
冷やす	*hiyasu*, to cool
冷たい	*tsumetai*, cold
温い	*atatakai*, warm
熱い	*atsui*, hot
熱	*netsu*, heat
油	*abura*, oil
水	*mizu*, water
冷水	*reisui*, cold water
湯	*yu*, hot water
熱湯	*nettō*, boiling water

4. RECIPES AND COOKING TIPS

Fish

The following information has been written for those who have not had much experience buying or cooking fish.

Fish with dark flesh tends to be stronger flavored and moister than fish with light or white flesh. Dark fish takes well to strong sauces. If your family does not like fish, cook a dark fish with a strong sauce rather than try to be inoffensive by cooking a mild fish in a mild sauce.

The flesh of larger fish tends to have larger flakes and will not seem as dry as the flesh of smaller fish. All fish is sensitive to cooking times and dries out quickly if overcooked. When cooking fish, check frequently by poking it gently with a fork. When the flesh separates easily, it is done.

All shellfish can be steamed, deep-fried, pan-fried, stewed, or cooked in chowder. Oily fish can be steamed, deep-fried, pan-fried, stewed, or broiled (if constantly basted with oil, butter, or a liquid). Lean fish is best steamed, but can also be deep-fried. Deep-fried fish must be coated beforehand with a batter, bread crumbs, or dry cornstarch to prevent excessive drying or disintegration. Oven roasting is recommended only for whole fish that have been immersed in a sauce of some kind.

One of the easiest ways to prepare fish is to steam it in the oven. Add a small amount of lemon juice, a dab of butter, and a sliced onion to the top of the raw fish. Put the fish in a baking pan and cover the entire pan with foil, or wrap individual portions in foil. Place in a hot oven for 10 to 20 minutes.

For a tasty, easy-to-make sauce, mince 1 garlic clove and put it in a small saucepan with 2 tablespoons of butter. Cook over medium heat until the garlic begins to turn slightly tan. Add 1 or 2 tablespoons of flour, stirring for a minute so that the flour does not burn. Then gradually add 1 can condensed chicken broth (such as Campbell's) to the flour and garlic, stirring briskly to prevent lumps. Cook over low to medium heat until thickened (about 5 minutes). Pour the sauce over the cooked fish.

Flour

A useful recipe conversion for flour is that 100 grams of flour is equivalent to $\frac{3}{4}$ American cup (180 cc.) less 2 tablespoons.

ALL-PURPOSE FLOUR: To start, when baking cakes and cookies, use 1 part cake flour to 3 parts bread flour. After trying that combination in a recipe, alter the proportions in later trials in the following manner: if the finished product should be more finely grained in texture, use a larger proportion of cake flour; if it should be more porous, use a larger proportion of bread flour.

SELF-RISING FLOUR: To make 1 cup of self-rising flour, use 1 scant American cup all-purpose flour, $\frac{1}{8}$ teaspoon salt, and between $1\frac{1}{4}$ and $1\frac{1}{2}$ teaspoon baking powder.

Frozen Foods

Label instructions for preparing frozen foods usually include fairly clear pictures. The major methods of preparation include the conventional oven, the microwave oven, pan frying, boiling, and steaming. For the conventional oven, next to a picture of an oven will be an indication of temperature (°C) and baking time (分 *fun,* minutes). For a microwave oven, only baking time, not temperature, will appear next to the picture of an oven.

If frying is recommended, a frying pan or wok will be pictured on the package accompanied by cooking time. For those foods packaged in plastic pouch bags that are to be immersed in boiling water, a saucepan of water and an indication of cooking time will appear on the package. For steaming, there will be a picture of a pot that looks like a steamer.

Gelatin

LEAF GELATIN: Heat $1\frac{1}{2}$ American cups (360 cc.) water in a saucepan. Add 4 tablespoons sugar; dissolve. Add 5 leaves of gelatin and stir the mixture over low heat until dissolved. Turn off heat. Assorted fruit can be added at this time. Chill 60 to 90 minutes.

POWDERED UNFLAVORED GELATIN: Add 1 packet (5 g.) gelatin to $\frac{4}{5}$ American cup (1 Japanese cup, or 200 cc.) hot water and stir until dissolved.

When using a recipe in American units calling for 1 envelope unflavored gelatin, substitute $2\frac{1}{3}$ 5-gram packets of Japanese powdered gelatin.

Noodles

To prepare dried or fresh uncooked noodles, most Japanese cookbooks say to bring water to a boil, add the noodles, stir and bring to a boil again, add a cup of cold water to reduce the boiling, bring to a boil again, add another cup of water, bring to a boil once more, cook at a low boil until done, and rinse well in a colander. Adding the cold water is recommended but not necessary. A large amount of sticky flour will adhere to the noodles unless they are rinsed thoroughly after being cooked.

Suggested cooking times are often indicated on the packages (look for the character 分 *fun,* minutes). It is probably best, however, to test the noodles as they are cooking.

Rice

WHITE RICE: For each cup of uncooked long-grain white rice you would normally start with, use 2 cups Japanese rice. (Use a Japanese cup-measure if you are using a rice cooker.) See how your family likes the rice and adjust the cooking amount accordingly.

TO WASH RICE: Put the rice into a deep bowl or pan. Run cold water into the pan, stir briefly, drain off most of the water, and stir the rice grains with your hand, a spoon, or a rice paddle *(shamoji)*. Repeat this procedure once. Then, run cold water into the pan, stir the rice in the water, and drain. Repeat this procedure as necessary until the drained water doesn't get any clearer with repeated rinsings.

TO COOK RICE ON THE STOVE: Use a heavy-bottomed saucepan with at least a 1-quart capacity for each cup of uncooked rice. In the pan put the washed and drained rice and an equal amount of water plus about 1 tablespoon extra water for each cup of rice. Let the rice and water stand for at least 30 minutes. (Alternately, put the washed and drained rice in a strainer for 30 minutes. Then put the rice and the appropriate amount of water into the saucepan and begin the cooking process without further waiting.) Cook, covered, over medium-high heat. When the water comes to a boil, reduce the heat to as low as possible and cook 10 minutes. Remove the pan from the heat and let it stand at least 10 minutes with the lid on. The rice will stay hot for at least 30 minutes if the lid is not removed. Before serving, fluff up the rice with a spoon, fork, or rice paddle.

The amount of cooking water required varies according to the variety of the rice and according to how recently the rice was harvested, but the above method will be safe for an initial try. Alter the proportions of water and rice to suit your taste and preference.

Cooking time may vary according to the stove flame and bottom thickness of the saucepan. If the rice is burned and undercooked when the lowest possible temperature is used, add more water and cook longer, or use a pan with a thicker bottom, or buy a rice cooker.

TO COOK WITH A RICE COOKER: Put the washed and drained rice, measured earlier with a Japanese cup-measure, into the rice cooker. Add water to the cooker, bringing the water level up to the numbered mark that corresponds to the number of cups of rice. Cover the cooker and let the water stand in it for at least 20 minutes (or for whatever time the maker of your rice cooker recommends). Put on the cooking switch. When the cooking process is finished, let the rice stand for 15 minutes covered. Open the lid and fluff up the rice with a spoon, fork, or rice paddle.

HAIGA RICE: Follow the instructions for white rice, above, but do not wash the rice.

BROWN RICE: Start with the same quantity of brown rice as that of Japanese white rice you normally use. Wash the rice briefly, then put it into a heavy-bottomed saucepan. (Except for certain models, rice cookers will not work for brown rice, since they are timed specifically for white rice.) For each cup of rice, add $1\frac{1}{2}$ to $1\frac{3}{4}$ cups water. Let the rice stand in the water for 20 minutes. Bring to a boil; reduce heat to as low as possible and simmer for approximately 30 minutes.

An interesting variation is to use 3 parts white rice to 1 part brown rice, following the instructions for cooking white rice. (The saucepan or rice-cooker method may be used for this variation.) The brown rice adds color to the dish, and because it has not been cooked as long as it should be, it adds a subtle texture to the rice.

Soybeans, fresh and frozen *(edamame)*

Bring to a boil enough salted water to cover the amount of fresh or frozen soybeans to be cooked. Add the soybeans, unshelled, to the water. Bring back to a boil; reduce heat to medium, cook, and start testing after about 6 minutes. The beans should be slightly crunchy, but not overly so, because when they are not cooked enough, the protein in them cannot be absorbed by the body. When the beans are done, rinse them in cold water and drain in a colander. Shell and eat.

Stir-Fry Recipe

The following is a basic recipe for use with meat alone, vegetables alone, or meat and vegetables together; any combination (including more than one kind of meat) is possible. The main points to remember are that the ingredients should be put in the pan according to the time each requires to cook, and that each food morsel should be small enough to eat without being cut at the table.

INGREDIENTS:

Meat: beef, chicken, lamb, pork; precooked or raw; ground, thinly sliced, slivered, or in small cubes

Vegetables: chopped garlic, finely chopped ginger, *naganegi,* or onion as a base; then any combination of the following: bamboo shoots, bean sprouts, broccoli, Brussels sprouts, cabbage, carrots, cauliflower, celery, *daikon,* lotus root, fresh or reconstituted dried mushrooms, shelled peas, snow peas, peppers

Liquid: beef bouillon, chicken broth, or *dashi;* hoisin sauce, *mirin* or cooking saké, *miso,* oyster sauce, sesame oil, soy sauce

Thickener (optional): corn starch or potato starch

Cooking oil

TO PREPARE:

1. Decide upon the proportion of vegetables and meat. Clean the vegetables, then chop, slice, or cut them into bite-size pieces. Long-cooking vegetables such as carrots should be cut into very thin strips or very small pieces. Experiment with different ways to cut vegetables and with different combinations.

2. Prepare meat by slicing or cutting into bite-size pieces.

3. Prepare the liquid: If you want a moister final product, prepare at least 1 cup bouillon, broth, or *dashi* in addition to the other liquids. Mix no more than three kinds of these other liquids; start with no more than 2 tablespoons of each thin liquid and 1 tablespoon of each thick liquid at first.

4. Prepare the thickener: Put about 1 tablespoon cornstarch or $\frac{1}{2}$ tablespoon potato starch in 1 tablespoon cold water and mix. Put all ingredients and liquids next to the cooking area, where they can be easily reached.

TO COOK:

1. Heat a wok or large frying pan over high heat to the count of 30. Add a few tablespoons oil and count to 30.

2. Add onions, garlic, or ginger and sauté for 1 minute. Move to the upper side of the wok.

3. Add the meat a small amount at a time and cook over high

heat until done (or until hot, if using precooked meat). Push the meat to the side of the wok.

4. Add the vegetable that cooks the longest. Cook 1 or 2 minutes until slightly wilted or slightly tender. Add the next vegetable, and so on, until all are lightly cooked. If the wok gets crowded, remove some of the food and continue cooking until all the ingredients are done. Then put everything back into the wok.

5. If bouillon, broth, or *dashi* is to be added, put this in with the meat and vegetables first and heat it until it begins to boil. (You may want to experiment with various amounts of liquid to suit your taste.) Add the other mixture of liquid seasonings. If thickener is to be used, restir the prepared starch-water mixture thoroughly, add to the wok, and stir until the sauce thickens. Serve.

⋊ RECOMMENDED READING

Adachi, Barbara C., ed. *Recipes from International Tokyo Tables.*
Tokyo: International Ladies Benevolent Society, 1982.
   The recipes in this cookbook form an impressive array of
international dishes all made by current or former residents
of Tokyo. The book also includes reproductions of twelve
prints published in 1860 and 1861 showing the Japanese view
of foreigners then living in Japan.

Condon, Camy, and Ashizawa, Sumiko. *The Japanese Guide to
Fish Cooking.* Tokyo: Shufunotomo, 1978.
   Excellent photographs of twenty kinds of raw fish, illus-
trations of fish preparation, and delicious recipes make this
book very helpful to the person who wants to cook fish in
Japan.

Itoh, Joan. *Rice Paddy Gourmet.* Tokyo: The Japan Times, 1976.
   Recipes and short essays on Japan are mixed with sea-
sonal themes. The recipes focus on using Japanese foods or
giving a Western touch to traditional Japanese dishes.

Japan External Trade Organization (JETRO). *Japan's Legal
Requirement for Foods and Additives.* Tokyo: Japan External
Trade Organization, 1981.
   This book outlines the Japanese laws concerning foods
and additives. An English copy is available in the sixth-
floor reading room of the JETRO offices, 2–2–5 Toranomon,
Minato-ku, Tokyo (the Kyodo News Building, diagonally

across from the American Embassy); telephone (03)–582–5511.

In the JETRO reading room is also a book that lists the ingredients of all foods sold in Japan. It is entitled *Shokuhin Yunyū no Jitsumu* (The business of food imports; 1980) and is published by Nihon Shokuhin Eisei Kyōkai (Japan food hygiene society). Domestic foods are covered in the appendix. The main categories in the text are in Japanese only, but the ingredients are listed in both Japanese and English.

Japan Travel Bureau. *Illustrated Eating in Japan*. Tokyo: Japan Travel Bureau, 1985.

This little book contains descriptions and illustrations of numerous Japanese dishes and their ingredients. It is very helpful for those interested in preparing and eating traditional Japanese foods.

Moriyama, Yukiko. *Quick and Easy Tofu Cook Book*. Tokyo: Joie, 1982.

This book, an easy way to get into tofu cooking, has excellent photographs accompanying its recipes.

Randolph, Elizabeth, and Overholser, Renee. *The Tofu–Miso High Efficiency Diet*. New York: Signet Books, 1981.

Explanations of tofu, *miso,* and seaweed are accompanied by data about nutrients and calories. The book includes traditional Japanese recipes.

Sakade, Florence, ed. *A Guide to Reading & Writing Japanese,* rev. ed. Tokyo: Charles E. Tuttle, 1961.

This book contains the kanji in general use at this time. There is an index by readings of the characters.

Tsuji, Shizuo. *Japanese Cooking: A Simple Art*. Tokyo: Kodansha International, 1980.

Shizuo Tsuji is the Julia Child of Japanese cuisine. The format of his book follows in style and detail Miss Child's two volumes of *Mastering the Art of French Cooking*. Illustrations are clear, recipes complete. The sections on utensils and ingredients are particularly helpful to anyone newly arrived in Japan.

Women's Group of the Tokyo American Club. *Itadakimasu.* Tokyo: Women's Group of the Tokyo American Club, 1984.

The recipes in this book are graded according to difficulty. Also included is helpful information about preparation, cooking times, measurements, and substitutions. Lively illustrations by Cleve Walker Washington enhance this work.

Women's Society, Tokyo Union Church. *Buy It and Try It.* Tokyo: Women's Society, Tokyo Union Church, 1979.

This book includes both Western and Japanese recipes, all written to be made in Japan. There are extensive glossaries of fish and other foods, and helpful hints for the non-Japanese resident. The book is also available in a Japanese-language edition.

✄ VOCABULARY LIST

This Vocabulary List gives the English, *rōmaji,* and kanji and kana for words and phrases concerned with food buying. Entries are listed according to general category (that is, the chapters of this book, beginning with Chapter 3). This arrangement corresponds approximately to how foods are displayed in a market. While shopping, you may turn the pages of the List to the category that corresponds to each section of your market.

The English terms are listed in the left-hand column and the Japanese (*rōmaji* and kanji/kana) in the right-hand column. Within each category, items are listed alphabetically according to the English terms, with the exception of some general terms that seemed best placed at the beginning of a category. As in the main text, the romanized Japanese word for an item has been inserted in the English alphabetical sequence if the Japanese word is considered primary.

How to Read a Food Label

additives	*tenkabutsu*	添加物
no additives	*mutenka*	無添加
care/caution in use	*shiyōjō no chūi*	使用上の注意
cooking instructions	*tsukuri-kata*	作り方
country of origin	*gensankokumei*	原産国名
China (People's Republic)	*Chūka Jimmin Kyōwakoku*	中華人民共和国 or *Chūgoku* 中国

China (Taiwan)　　　　　*Chūka Minkoku, Taiwan-shō* 中華民国台湾省

Hong Kong　　　　　　*Honkon* 香港

date of:

 import　　　　　　*yunyū nengappi* 輸入年月日

 manufacture　　　　*seizō nengappi* 製造年月日

 packaging　　　　　*kakō nengappi* 加工年月日

distributor　　　　　　*hatsubai-moto* 発売元

importer　　　　　　　*yunyūgyōsha* 輸入業者

ingredients　　　　　　*genzairyōmei* 原材料名

 artificial color　　　*gōsei chakushokuryō* 合成着色料

 artificial flavoring　*chakkōryō* 着香料

 artificial preservative　*gōsei hozonryō* 合成保存料

 artificial sweetener　*gōsei kammiryō* 合成甘味料

 monosodium glutamate (msg.)　*kagaku chōmiryō* 化学調味料

 natural　　　　　　*tennen* 天然

 salt　　　　　　　*shio* 塩 or *shokuen* 食塩

 sugar　　　　　　　*satō* 砂糖

 synthetic (artificial)　*gōsei* 合成

instant　　　　　　　*sokuseki* 即席

manufacturer　　　　　*seizōsha* 製造者

measurement units:

 gram (g.)　　　　　*guramu* グラム

 kilogram (kg.)　　　*kiroguramu* キログラム

 milliliter (ml.)　　　*miririttoru* ミリリットル

 liter (l.)　　　　　　*rittoru* リットル

method of:

 handling　　　　　*tori-atsukaijō no chūi* 取り扱い上の注意

 preparation　　　　*chōri hōhō* 調理方法 or *meshiagarikata* 召し上り方

 use　　　　　　　　*shiyō hōhō* 使用方法

name of product　　　　*himmei* 品名

net weight or volume:

in information panel	*naiyōryō* 内容量
on preprinted labels	*shōmiyrō* 正味量
no agricultural chemicals	*munōyaku saibai* 無農薬栽培
no-brand	*mujirushi* 無印
number of:	
packets enclosed	*～fukuro-iri* ～袋入
portions	*～ko-iri* ～個入/～コ入
servings	*～nimbun* ～人分 or
	～nimmae ～人前 or
	～sarabun ～皿分
price:	
net	*nedan* 値段 or *kakaku* 価格
per 100 grams	*hyaku guramu atari,* 100 g. 当り
seller	*hambaisha* 販売者
storage information	*hozonhōhō* 保存方法 or
	hozonjō no chūi 保存上の注意
"to be eaten by this date"	*shōmi kigen* 賞味期限 or
	shōmi kijitsu 賞味期日
"to be eaten within this period"	*shōmi kikan* 賞味期間
yen	*en* 円 or ¥

Baking Needs and Spices

baking powder	*bēkingu paudā* ベーキング パウダー
baking soda (bicarbonate of soda)	*bēkingu sōda* ベーキング ソーダ or
	tansan suiso natoryūmu 炭酸水素ナトリウム or
	jūsō 重曹
chocolate (baking)	*chokorēto* チョコレート
chocolate chips	*chokorēto chippusu* チョコレート チップス
cocoa	*kokoa* ココア
extracts	*essensu* エッセンス
almond oil	*āmondo oiru* アーモンド オイル

banana	*banana* バナナ
lemon	*remon* レモン
melon	*meron* メロン
orange	*orenji* オレンジ
pineapple	*painappuru* パイナップル
strawberry	*sutoroberii* ストロベリー
vanilla	*banira* バニラ
gelatin	*zerachin* ゼラチン
leaf	*riifu* リーフ
powdered	*paudā* パウダー
spices	*kōshinryō* 香辛料
cayenne pepper	*(ichimi) tōgarashi* （一味）唐辛子/とうがらし
coarsely ground	*arabiki* あらびき
curry powder	*karē-ko* カレー粉
garlic	*gārikku* ガーリック
ginger	*shōga* しょうが
horseradish (Japanese)	*wasabi* わさび
kurogoma shio (black sesame seeds and salt)	黒ごましお
mustard	*karashi* からし
pepper	*koshō* コショウ
powdered	*kona-/-ko* 〜粉〜
sanshō (prickly pear)	山椒/さんしょう
sesame seeds	*goma* 胡麻/ごま
shichimi tōgarashi (seven-spice pepper)	七味とうがらし
whole (as peppercorns)	*tsubu* 粒
yeast (dry)	*dorai iisuto* ドライ イースト

Bread, Cereal, and Pasta

bean jam	*an* あん
bread	*pan* パン

Dairy Products and Margarine

INFORMATION PANEL AND LABEL:

classification	*shuruibetsu* 種類別
composition	*seibun* 成分
ingredients	*shiyō genryō* 使用原料 or
	genryōmei 原料名 or
	shuyōkongōbutsu 主要混合物
no additives	*seibun muchōsei* 成分無調整

INGREDIENTS AND ADDITIVES:

animal fat	*dōbutsu-yushi* 動物油脂
beta-carotene	*beta-karochin* β-カロチン
butterfat	*nyūshibō* 乳脂肪
casein	*kazein* カゼイン
corn syrup	*kōn shiroppu* コーン シロップ
emulsifier	*nyūkazai* 乳化剤
flavoring	*kōryō* 香料
linoleic acid	*rinōrusan* リノール酸
non-fat milk powder	*dasshi-funnyū* 脱脂粉乳
non-fat milk solids	*mushinyū-kokei* 無脂乳固形
percentage of	*-bun* ～分
salt	*shio* 塩 or *shokuen* 食塩
salt free	*muen* 無塩
sugar	*satō* 砂糖
vegetable oil	*shokubutsuyu* 食物油
vitamin	*bitamin* ビタミン
butter	*batā* バター
cheese	*chiizu* チーズ
processed	*purosesu chiizu* プロセス チーズ
smoked	*sumōku chiizu* スモーク チーズ
cottage cheese	*kattēji chiizu* カッテージ チーズ
cream	*kuriimu* クリーム
cream cheese	*kuriimu chiizu* クリーム チーズ
ice cream	*aisu kuriimu* アイス クリーム
chocolate	*chokorēto* チョコレート
coffee	*kōhii* コーヒー
peach	*momo* 桃/もも or *piichi* ピーチ

strawberry	*ichigo* いちご or *sutoroberii* ストロベリー
vanilla	*banira* バニラ
margarine	*māgarin* マーガリン
corn oil	*kōn abura* コーン油 or *tōmorokoshi abura* とうもろこし油
palm oil	*pāmu abura* パーム油
safflower oil	*benibana abura* 紅花油 or *safurawā abura* サフラワー油
soybean oil	*daizu abura* 大豆油
sunflower oil	*himawari abura* 向日葵油/ひまわり油 or *sanfurawā abura* サンフラワー油
milk	*gyūnyū* 牛乳 or *miruku* ミルク
condensed	*kondensu miruku* コンデンスミルク
evaporated	*ebamiruku* エバミルク
low-fat	*rōfatto miruku* ローファットミルク
milk beverage	*nyūinryō* 乳飲料
powdered whole	*zenshi-funnyū* 全脂粉乳
processed	*kakōnyū* 加工乳
skim	*sukimu miruku* スキムミルク
soybean	*tōnyū* 豆乳
sour cream	*sawā kuriimu* サワークリーム
yogurt	*yōguruto* ヨーグルト
plain	*purēn* プレーン

Fish and Seafood

barracuda	*kamasu* かます
bonito	*katsuo* 鰹/かつお
carp	*koi* 鯉/こい
cod	*tara* 鱈/たら
flounder	*karei* 鰈/かれい
halibut	*hirame* 平目/ひらめ

herring	*nishin* 鰊/鯡/にしん
horse mackerel	*aji* 鯵/あじ
katsuobushi (bonito shavings)	かつおぶし
lobster	*ise-ebi* 伊勢海老
mackerel	*saba* 鯖/さば
octopus	*tako* たこ
oysters	*kaki* かき
for eating raw	*seishoku-yō* 生食用
perch	*kisu* 鱚/きす
pike	*samma* さんま
prawn	*kuruma-ebi* 車海老
river trout	*ayu* 鮎/あゆ
salmon	*sake* 鮭/さけ or *shake* しゃけ
fresh	*nama-jake* 生じゃけ
heavily salted	*shio-jake* 塩じゃけ
lightly salted	*ama-jio* 甘塩
smoked	*sumōku sāmon* スモーク サーモン
sardines	*iwashi* 鰯/いわし
sashimi (sliced fish for eating raw)	刺身/さしみ
sea bass	*suzuki* 鱸/すずき
sea bream	*tai* 鯛/たい
shrimp	*ebi* 海老/えび
squid	*ika* いか
swordfish	*mekajiki* めかじき
trout	*masu* 鱒/ます
tuna	*maguro* 鮪/まぐろ
pink flesh	*chūtoro* 中とろ
white flesh	*toro* とろ
yellowtail	*buri* 鰤/ぶり
hamachi (young stage of yellowtail)	はまち

Flour

INFORMATION PANEL AND LABEL:

kind	*shurui* 種類
main uses	*omo na yōto* 主な用途
bread	*pan* パン
cake	*kēki* ケーキ
cookies	*kukkii* クッキー
hand-made *udon* (noodles)	*teuchi udon* 手打ちうどん
pizza	*pittsa* ピッツァ or *piza* ピザ
rolls	*rōru* ロール
tempura (batter fry)	天ぷら
traditional sweets	*okashi* お菓子
unbleached	*muhyōhaku* 無漂白
cornstarch	*kōn sutāchi* コーン スターチ
potato starch	*katakuri-ko* 片栗粉
tempura (batter fry) flour	*tempura-ko* 天ぷら粉
wheat flour	*komugi-ko* 小麦粉
hard-wheat (bread)	*kyōryoku-ko* 強力粉
soft-wheat (cake)	*hakuriki-ko* 薄力粉

Frozen Food

frozen food	*reitō shokuhin* 冷凍食品
green soybeans	*edamame* 枝豆/えだ豆

Juice

fruit juice	*kajū* 果汁
less than	*miman* 未満
mandarin orange; tangerine	*mikan* みかん
Valencia orange	*barenshia orenji* バレンシア オレンジ

Meat

LABEL:

high-grade	*jō* 上
imported	*yunyū* 輸入
middle-grade	*chū* 中

KINDS:

bacon	*bēkon*	ベーコン
beef	*gyūniku*	牛肉
domestic	*wagyū*	和牛
chicken	*toriniku*	鶏肉/鳥肉
young	*wakadori*	若鶏/若鳥
duck	*kamo*	鴨/かも or *ahiru* あひる
ham	*hamu*	ハム
lamb	*ramu*	ラム
mutton	*maton*	マトン
pork	*butaniku*	豚肉
turkey	*shichimenchō*	七面鳥
veal	*ko-ushi*	仔牛

CUTS OF BEEF, PORK, AND LAMB:

abdomen	*bara*	ばら
chops	*kirimi*	切身
fillet (tenderloin)	*hire*	ヒレ
ground	*hikiniku*	挽肉
ground beef and pork	*gyūbuta hikiniku*	牛豚挽肉 or
mixture	*aibiki*	合挽
leg	*momo*	もも/モモ
liver	*rebā*	レバー
roast	*rōsuto*	ロースト
shoulder	*kata*	肩/かた
sirloin	*rōsu*	ロース
spare ribs	*supea ribu*	スペア リブ
tongue	*tan*	タン

CUTS OF CHICKEN:

bone in	*honetsuki*	骨付
boneless breast without skin	*sasami sujinashi*	ささみすじなし
boneless meat with skin	*shōniku*	正肉
breast	*mune*	胸/むね/ムネ

gizzards	*suna-gimo* すなぎも
ground	*hikiniku* 挽肉
internal organs	*motsu* もつ
leg	*momo* もも/モモ
liver	*kimo* きも or *rebā* レバー
lower wing	*tebasaki* 手羽さき
upper wing	*tebamoto* 手羽もと

METHODS OF PREPARATION:

barbeque	*bābekyū* バーベキュー or *yakiniku* 焼肉
Korean style	*karubiyaki* カルビ焼
grill	*amiyaki* あみやき
sauté	*sotē* ソテー or *yakiniku* 焼肉
in butter	*batayaki* バタ焼
shabu-shabu (a cook-at-the-table dish)	しゃぶしゃぶ
steak	*sutēki* ステーキ
stew	*shichū* シチュー
sukiyaki	*sukiyaki* すき焼

Oil and Shortening

oil	*abura/yu* 油
blended	*shokuyō chōgō abura* 食用調合油
corn	*kōn abura* コーン油 or *tōmorokoshi abura* とうもろこし油
cottonseed	*menjitsu-yu* 綿実油
palm	*pāmu abura* パーム油
rapeseed	*natane abura* 菜種油/なたね油
safflower	*benibana abura* 紅花油 or *safurawā abura* サフラワー油
salad	*sarada abura* サラダ油
sesame	*goma abura* ごま油
soybean	*daizu abura* 大豆油

sunflower	*himawari abura* 向日葵油/ひまわり油 or *sanfurawā abura* サンフラワー油
tempura (batter fry)	*tempura abura* 天ぷら油
vegetable	*shokubutsuyu* 植物油
shortening	*shōtoningu* ショートニング

Produce

FRUIT:

apples	*ringo* りんご
cooking	*ryōri-yō no ringo* 料理用のりんご
bananas	*banana* バナナ
blueberries	*burūberii* ブルーベリー
cherries	*sakurambo* 桜んぼ/さくらんぼ
citrons	*yuzu* ゆず
cranberries	*kuranberii* クランベリー
figs	*ichijiku* いちじく
grapefruit	*gurēpufurūtsu* グレープフルーツ
grapes	*budō* 葡萄/ぶどう
kiwifruit	*kiiui* キーウィ or *kiiuifurūtsu* キーウィフルーツ
lemons	*remon* レモン
litchis	*reishi* れいし
loquats	*biwa* びわ
mandarin oranges	*mikan* みかん
mangoes	*mangō* マンゴー
melons	*meron* メロン
"prince"	*purinsu* プリンス
mikan (mandarin orange; tangerine)	みかん
nashi (pear-apple)	梨/なし
nijusseiki (yellow-skinned variety of *nashi*)	二十世紀

oranges	*orenji* オレンジ
papayas	*papaiya* パパイヤ
peaches	*momo* 桃/もも
pears	*seiyō nashi* 西洋なし
persimmons	*kaki* 柿/かき
dried	*hoshi-gaki* ほし柿
pineapples	*painappuru* パイナップル
plums	*puramu* プラム
pomegranates	*zakuro* ざくろ
raspberries	*razuberii* ラズベリー
strawberries	*ichigo* 苺/いちご
tangerines	*mikan* みかん
ume (green plums for wine and pickling)	梅
watermelon	*suika* 西瓜/すいか

VEGETABLES:

asparagus	*asuparagasu* アスパラガス
bamboo shoots	*takenoko* 竹の子/たけのこ
bean sprouts	*moyashi* もやし
broad beans	*soramame* そら/豆
broccoli	*burokkorii* ブロッコリー
Brussels sprouts	*mekyabetsu* 芽キャベツ
burdock	*gobō* ごぼう
cabbage	*kyabetsu* キャベツ
carrots	*ninjin* 人参/にんじん
cauliflower	*karifurawā* カリフラワー
celery	*serorii* セロリー
chestnuts	*kuri* 栗
Chinese cabbage	*hakusai* 白菜
cilantro (fresh coriander)	*kosai* コサイ
corn	*tōmorokoshi* とうもろこし
cucumbers	*kyūri* きゅうり
daikon (long white radish)	大根
eggplant	*nasu* なす
garlic	*ninniku* にんにく

garlic stems	*ninniku no kuki* にんにくの茎
ginger	*shōga* しょうが
ginkgo nuts	*ginnan* ぎんなん
horse beans	*soramame* そら豆
kaiware (young shoots of *daikon*)	かいわれ
komatsuna (leafy green vegetable)	小松菜
leeks	*riiku* リーク
lettuce	*retasu* レタス
lotus root	*renkon* 蓮根
mushrooms	*kinoko* 茸/きのこ or *take* 茸/たけ
button	*masshurūmu* マッシュルーム
enoki	えのき
matsutake	松茸/まつたけ
shiitake	椎茸/しいたけ
naganegi (long green onion)	長ねぎ
nira (leeklike vegetable)	にら
onions	*tamanegi* 玉ねぎ
red	*akanegi* 赤ねぎ
peas	*endōmame* えんどう豆
peppers, green	*piiman* ピーマン
shishitō (small variety of pepper)	ししとう
perilla (beefsteak leaf)	*shiso* しそ
potatoes	*imo* 芋/いも
naga-imo (long yam)	長いも
taro	*sato-imo* 里芋 or *taro* たろ/タロ
white	*jaga-imo* 馬鈴薯/じゃがいも
yama-imo (irregularly shaped yam)	山芋/山いも
pumpkin	*kabocha* かぼちゃ
radishes	*radishu* ラディシュ
rape blossoms	*nanohana* 菜の花
snow peas	*saya-endō* さやえんどう

soybeans, green	*edamame* 技豆/えだ豆
spikenard	*udo* うど
spinach	*hōrensō* ほうれん草
spring chrysanthemums	*shungiku* 春菊/しゅんぎく
squash	*kabocha* かぼちゃ
string beans	*saya-ingen* さやいんげん
sweet potatoes	*satsuma-imo* さつまいも
tomatoes	*tomato* トマト
trefoil	*mitsuba* 三ッ葉
turnips	*kabu* かぶ
wasabi (Japanese horserad-ish)	わさび

Rice

brown rice	*gemmai* 玄米
haiga (germ) rice	*haiga seimai* 胚芽精米
uncooked rice	*kome* 米/こめ
white rice	*hakumai* 白米
koshihikari (a high-grade variety)	コシヒカリ
sasanishiki (a high-grade variety)	ササニシキ

Salt and Sugar

ajishio (salt and msg. mix-ture)	アジシオ
monosodium glutamate (msg.)	*kagaku chōmiryō* 化学調味料
salt	*shio* 塩 or *shokuen* 食塩
cooking and general use	*katei-yō shio* 家庭用塩 or *shokuen* 食塩
refined	*seisei-en* 精製塩
table	*shokutaku-en* 食卓塩
salt-substitute ingredients:	
potassium chloride	*enka karyūmu* 塩化カリウム
sodium chloride	*enka natoryūmu* 塩化ナトリウム

sugar	*satō*	砂糖
brown	*buraun shugā*	ブラウン シュガー
for coffee	*kohii-yō shugā*	コーヒー用シュガー
confectioners'	*funtō*	粉糖
cube	*kaku-zatō*	角砂糖
granulated	*guranyū-tō*	グラニュー糖
rock	*kōri-zatō*	氷砂糖
shiro-zatō (moist white sugar for cooking)		白砂糖

Tea

barley tea	*mugicha*	麦茶
black tea	*kōcha*	紅茶
Chinese tea:		
jasmine	*jasumincha*	ジャスミン茶
oolong	*ūroncha*	烏龍茶/ウーロン茶
Japanese (green) tea	*ocha*	お茶
bancha (third-grade tea)		番茶
gemmaicha (tea mixed with rice kernels)		玄米茶
gyokuro (top-grade tea)		玉露
hōjicha (roasted tea)		ほうじ茶
matcha (powdered tea)		抹茶
sencha (second-grade tea)		煎茶/せん茶
shincha (new tea leaves)		新茶

Vinegar and Sauces

ketchup	*kechappu*	ケチャップ
mayonnaise	*mayonēzu*	マヨネーズ
meat sauces:		
medium thickness	*chūkoi*	中濃
tonkatsu sōsu (thickest; for pork cutlet)		とんかつ ソース
Worcestershire	*usutā sōsu*	ウスター ソース

mustard	*masutādo* マスタード or *yō-garashi* 洋がらし
vinegar	*su* 酢
cider	*ringo-su* りんご酢
citron	*pon-zu* ぽん酢
plain (grain)	*su* 酢 or *kokumotsu-su* 穀物酢
rice	*yone-zu/kome-zu* 米酢
for *sushi*	*sushi-zu* すし酢
wine	*wain binegā* ワイン ビネガー

Traditional Foods

dashi (soup stock)	出し/だし
fish paste	*nerimono* 練りもの
chikuwa	ちくわ
hampen	はんぺん
kamaboko	かまぼこ
satsuma-age	さつまあげ
fu (wheat gluten)	ふ
namafu (fresh wheat gluten)	生ふ
konnyaku (devil's tongue jelly)	こんにゃく
shirataki (*konnyaku* in string form)	白滝/しらたき
miso	味噌/みそ
amamiso (light *miso*)	甘みと
chōgō miso (blended *miso*)	調合みそ
karamiso (dark *miso*)	辛みと
komemiso (rice *miso*)	米みそ
mamemiso (soybean *miso*)	豆みそ
mugimiso (barley *miso*)	麦みそ
shiromiso (very light *miso*)	白みそ
noodles	*menrui* 麺類/めん類
buckwheat	*soba* そば
Chinese	*Chūka soba* 中華そば

rāmen	ラーメン
yakisoba (fried noodles)	焼そば
hiyamugi	ひやむぎ
kishimen	きしめん
sōmen	そうめん
udon	うどん
saké	*sake* 酒 or *Nihonshu* 日本酒
cooking	*ryōri-yō no sake* 料理用の酒
for drinking:	
special grade	*tokkyūshu* 特級酒
first grade	*ikkyūshu* 一級酒
second grade	*nikyūshu* 二級酒
mirin (sweet cooking saké)	みりん
seaweed	*kaisō* 海草
hijiki	ひじき
kelp	*kombu* 昆布/こんぶ
dashikombu (kelp used for soup stock)	だしこんぶ
nikombu (kelp used in cooking)	煮こんぶ
laver	*nori* 海苔/のり
ajitsuke-nori (flavored laver)	味付のり
aonori (flaked laver)	青のり
yakinori (unflavored laver)	焼のり
wakame	わかめ
soy sauce	*shōyu* 醤油/しょうゆ
koikuchi (thick)	濃口/こいくち
low salt	*usu-jio* うす塩
very low salt	*gen'en* 減塩
usukuchi (thin)	うすくち
tofu (soybean curd)	*tōfu* 豆腐/とうふ
abura-age (deep-fried, thin tofu)	油揚/油あげ

gammodoki or *gammo*   がんもどき or がんも
  (deep-fried tofu with
  other ingredients)
kinu-dōfu or *kinu-goshi*   絹豆腐 or 絹ごし
  or *kinu* (silk)   or 絹/きぬ
momen (cotton) or   木綿/もめん or 綿豆腐
  mendōfu
nama-age (deep-fried,   生揚
  thick tofu)
okara (white, fluffy by-   おから
  product)
yaki-dōfu (seared tofu)   焼どうふ/やきどうふ

Household Needs: Non-edibles

INFORMATION PANEL:

composition	*seibun*	成分
name of product	*himmei*	品名
pH	*ekisei*	液性
neutral	*chūsei*	中性
weak alkali	*jaku-arukari-sei*	弱アルカリ性
uses	*yōto*	用途

LABEL:

abrasives	*kemmazai*	けんま剤
detergent	*kaimenkasseizai*	界面活性剤
chlorine	*jia-ensosan natoryūmu*	次亜塩素酸ナトリウム
granular	*tsubu*	粒
liquid	*ekitai*	液体
powdered	*kona*	紛
aluminum foil	*aruminyūmu hoiru*	アルミニューム ホイル
anti-static spray	*irui no seidenki bōshi*	衣類の静電気防止

bags:
  food storage   *pori-bukuro* ポリ袋
  freezer use   *reitō-yō* 冷凍用
  garbage   *gomi-bukuro* ゴミ袋
bathroom cleaner   *yokushitsu-yō senjōzai* 浴室用洗
                       浄剤

bleach   *hyōhakuzai* 漂白剤
  for colored clothes   *iromono-yō* 色物用
  kitchen   *kitchin* キッチン
    tableware   *shokki* 食器
  laundry   *sentaku-yō* 洗濯用/洗たく用
cleanser   *kurenzā* クレンザー
detergent   *gōseisenzai* 合成洗剤
  dish   *daidokoro-yō gōseisenzai* 台所
                       用合成洗剤

  dishwasher   *zenjidō shokki araiki-yō gōseisen-zai* 全自動食器洗い機用合成
                       洗剤

  household   *jūtaku-yō senzai* 住宅用洗剤 or
                       jūtaku-yō matawa kagu-yō gōsei-senzai
                       住宅用又は家具用合成洗剤

  laundry   *gōseisenzai-kei sentakuzai* 合成
                       洗剤系洗濯剤 or
                       sentaku-yō gōseisenzai 洗濯用合
                       成洗剤

drain cleaner   *haisuipaipu-yō senjōzai* 排水パ
                       イプ用洗浄剤

fabric softener   *jūnan shiagezai* 柔軟仕上げ剤
laundry starch   *sentaku nori* 洗濯糊
paper napkins   *kami napukin* 紙ナプキン
paper towels   *pēpā taoru* ペーパータオル
plastic wrap   *rappu firumu* ラップ フィルム
tissues   *tishū* ティシュー
toilet cleaner   *toiretto-yō senjōzai* トイレット
                       用洗浄剤

toilet deodorant	*toire shōshū-eki*	トイレ消臭液
toilet paper	*toiretto pēpā*	トイレット ペーパー or
	toiretto tishū	トイレット ティシュー

⚡ INDEX